OPPOSING
VIEWPOINTS®
SERIES

stry

DISCARDED

Children and the
Entertainment Industry

Other Books of Related Interest:

Opposing Viewpoints Series

Obesity

At Issue Series

Beauty Pageants

Current Controversies Series

Media Ethics

"Congress shall make no law . . . abridging the freedom of speech, or of the press."

First Amendment to the U.S. Constitution

The basic foundation of our democracy is the First Amendment guarantee of freedom of expression. The Opposing Viewpoints Series is dedicated to the concept of this basic freedom and the idea that it is more important to practice it than to enshrine it.

OPPOSING
VIEWPOINTS®
SERIES

Children and the Entertainment Industry

Karen Miller, book editor

GREENHAVEN PRESS
A part of Gale, Cengage Learning

GALE
CENGAGE Learning™

Detroit • New York • San Francisco • New Haven, Conn • Waterville, Maine • London

GALE
CENGAGE Learning

Christine Nasso, *Publisher*
Elizabeth Des Chenes, *Managing Editor*

For more information, contact:
Greenhaven Press
27500 Drake Rd.
Farmington Hills, MI 48331-3535
Or you can visit our Internet site at gale.cengage.com

LIBRARY OF CONGRESS CATALOGING-IN-PUBLICATION DATA

Children and the entertainment industry / Karen Miller, book editor.
    p. cm. -- (Opposing viewpoints)
Includes bibliographical references and index.
    ISBN 978-0-7377-4763-8 (hardcover) -- ISBN 978-0-7377-4764-5 (pbk.)
    1. Television and children. 2. Child actors. 3. Performing arts. I. Miller, Karen, 1973-
    HQ784.T4C493 2010
    302.23'45083--dc22

                                                         2009050445

Printed in the United States of America
1 2 3 4 5 6 7 14 13 12 11 10

Contents

Chapter 3: Are Children in the Entertainment Industry Exploited?

Chapter 4: What Role Do Parents Play in Their Children's Careers in Entertainment?

Why Consider Opposing Viewpoints?

> *"The only way in which a human being can make some approach to knowing the whole of a subject is by hearing what can be said about it by persons of every variety of opinion and studying all modes in which it can be looked at by every character of mind. No wise man ever acquired his wisdom in any mode but this."*
>
> John Stuart Mill

In our media-intensive culture it is not difficult to find differing opinions. Thousands of newspapers and magazines and dozens of radio and television talk shows resound with differing points of view. The difficulty lies in deciding which opinion to agree with and which "experts" seem the most credible. The more inundated we become with differing opinions and claims, the more essential it is to hone critical reading and thinking skills to evaluate these ideas. Opposing Viewpoints books address this problem directly by presenting stimulating debates that can be used to enhance and teach these skills. The varied opinions contained in each book examine many different aspects of a single issue. While examining these conveniently edited opposing views, readers can develop critical thinking skills such as the ability to compare and contrast authors' credibility, facts, argumentation styles, use of persuasive techniques, and other stylistic tools. In short, the Opposing Viewpoints Series is an ideal way to attain the higher-level thinking and reading skills so essential in a culture of diverse and contradictory opinions.

In addition to providing a tool for critical thinking, Opposing Viewpoints books challenge readers to question their own strongly held opinions and assumptions. Most people form their opinions on the basis of upbringing, peer pressure, and personal, cultural, or professional bias. By reading carefully balanced opposing views, readers must directly confront new ideas as well as the opinions of those with whom they disagree. This is not to simplistically argue that everyone who reads opposing views will—or should—change his or her opinion. Instead, the series enhances readers' understanding of their own views by encouraging confrontation with opposing ideas. Careful examination of others' views can lead to the readers' understanding of the logical inconsistencies in their own opinions, perspective on why they hold an opinion, and the consideration of the possibility that their opinion requires further evaluation.

Evaluating Other Opinions

To ensure that this type of examination occurs, Opposing Viewpoints books present all types of opinions. Prominent spokespeople on different sides of each issue as well as well-known professionals from many disciplines challenge the reader. An additional goal of the series is to provide a forum for other, less known, or even unpopular viewpoints. The opinion of an ordinary person who has had to make the decision to cut off life support from a terminally ill relative, for example, may be just as valuable and provide just as much insight as a medical ethicist's professional opinion. The editors have two additional purposes in including these less known views. One, the editors encourage readers to respect others' opinions—even when not enhanced by professional credibility. It is only by reading or listening to and objectively evaluating others' ideas that one can determine whether they are worthy of consideration. Two, the inclusion of such viewpoints encourages the important critical thinking skill of objectively evaluating an author's credentials and bias. This evaluation will illuminate an author's reasons for taking a particular stance on an issue and will aid in readers' evaluation of the author's ideas.

It is our hope that these books will give readers a deeper understanding of the issues debated and an appreciation of the complexity of even seemingly simple issues when good and honest people disagree. This awareness is particularly important in a democratic society such as ours in which people enter into public debate to determine the common good. Those with whom one disagrees should not be regarded as enemies but rather as people whose views deserve careful examination and may shed light on one's own.

Thomas Jefferson once said that "difference of opinion leads to inquiry, and inquiry to truth." Jefferson, a broadly educated man, argued that "if a nation expects to be ignorant and free . . . it expects what never was and never will be." As individuals and as a nation, it is imperative that we consider the opinions of others and examine them with skill and discernment. The Opposing Viewpoints Series is intended to help readers achieve this goal.

David L. Bender and Bruno Leone,
Founders

Introduction

> *"There's only one person in the whole world exactly like you, and people can like you just because you're you."*
>
> —Fred Rogers
> as "Mr. Rogers,"
> Mister Rogers' Neighborhood,
> 1968–2001.

Don Chance, a professor of finance at Louisiana State University, blames a lot of problems with present-day college students on the television program, *Mister Rogers' Neighborhood*. In a 2007 article written by Jeffrey Zaslow, "Blame It on Mr. Rogers: Why Young Adults Feel So Entitled," Chance describes the crowds of students who approach him asking for enough extra points to get an A grade for his course. He characterizes them as narcissists suffering from a sense of entitlement, who believe they should be rewarded for showing up to class as much as for working hard to earn good grades. He contrasts this group of people to students born and raised in Asia—students who did not watch *Mister Rogers' Neighborhood* on television—who work hard and consider a B or C grade a challenge to improve, not the denial of a grade that is owed to them. According to Chance, the "culture of excessive doting" found a national spokesman in Fred Rogers, who told too many kids that they were special and gave them the wrong ideas about how to succeed in the adult world.

This claim met immediate argument. Fred Rogers, the man as well as the character "Mr. Rogers" from his television show, was a beloved father figure to millions of children around the world. *Mister Rogers' Neighborhood* aired every weekday on public television from 1968 to 2001, and Rogers is noted as a tireless children's advocate, who traveled extensively from public appearances, to congressional hearings, to the production studio. He designed a show that respected children's point of view and directly addressed their concerns, fears, questions, and triumphs. Joyce Millman, a Salon.com television critic from 1995–2001, is a strong supporter of his program. Her 1999 article about Rogers and his accomplishments describes *Mister Rogers' Neighborhood* as thirty minutes of "peace, calm, familiarity and safety," when "troubling feelings are gently explored," in a program that is created just to share love with its audience. The show balances fantasy and reality. It is punctuated with predictable and comforting rituals and sends a message to children that they are likable, interesting people and that there are adults who understand and care for them.

Rogers did believe that children were special and should be treated accordingly, but he believed that they needed programming designed for their particular needs—not that all programming should be appropriate for a child audience. He told children they were special because of their individuality and because they were people, too—not that they were special because they were children. To his supporters, the distinctions are crystal clear. To supporters of Don Chance's arguments, Rogers is the face of a trend that subordinates adult needs to juvenile ones, in all aspects of life.

The claim that the entertainment industry can damage an entire generation of young children can be debated, but the entertainment industry is certainly extremely pervasive in modern life. The suggestion that *Mister Rogers' Neighborhood* has turned children into narcissists is simply the latest addition to claims of the damaging effects of the media. Over the years, MTV has been accused of shortening attention spans, video games of increasing aggression, magazines of encouraging eating disorders, clothing manufacturers of sexualizing teens, and Tinky Winky the Teletubby of promoting a gay agenda. At some point in time, just about every social, biological, or educational problem with children has been attributed to some form of entertainment. On the one hand, it hardly seems fair to blame the creators and producers of manufacturing social ills when they only set out to give kids something fun to do in their free time. On the other hand, kids spend so much time engaged in entertainment (often without adult supervision) and have such relatively poor judgment (because of their age and lack of experience), that it makes perfect sense that they would be unduly influenced by the images they see and the games they play. Every generation adapts to the technology and knowledge of their age; in an era when information and entertainment are inextricably linked, the entertainment industry is going to have a much larger effect in the development of children's lives. Whether that effect is noticeable, measurable, or even definable, on the personal, cultural, or political scale, is a question that will likely inspire discussion and controversy for many years to come.

Opposing Viewpoints: Children and the Entertainment Industry addresses some of the ways that the entertainment industry affects children's lives. Its four chapters, What Messages Does the Entertainment Industry Send to Children? How Does the Entertainment Industry Engage Children? Are Children in the Entertainment Industry Exploited? and What Role Do Parents Play in Their Children's Careers in Entertainment? identify many of the ways that the content of the entertainment that children consume and create have a direct impact on how children understand themselves, adults, and the world they share.

OPPOSING
VIEWPOINTS®
SERIES

CHAPTER 1

What Messages Does the Entertainment Industry Send to Children?

Chapter Preface

Reality television is an art form that audiences and critics love to hate. Lambasted by some for their exaggerated drama and staged artificiality, they nonetheless enjoy a position of power on network and cable schedules. Thousands of people dream of appearing on one; the very lucky ones even end up with their own shows—an admitted mixed blessing. Jon and Kate Gosselin of *Jon & Kate Plus 8* attribute their divorce in part to the burdens of living with television crews; smaller tragedies occur more frequently. Contestants on competition shows like *Survivor* and *Project Runway* often report shock at how horribly they are portrayed by show editors for the sake of creating tension between participants and thus suspense for the audience.

A study conducted in the United Kingdom, however, finds a surprising result about reality television programming and content. The organization Women in Journalism conducted research and presented it at the "Hoodies or Altar Boys?" summit, in March 2009. It concerned the effect of negative portrayals of teenage boys in the media on teenage boys' perceptions of their safety and of each other. Eighty-five percent of boys surveyed agreed with the statement that the news media presented them in a bad light to the rest of the public. In contrast, less than 20 percent of boys surveyed thought that reality television portrayed them negatively. Whereas news media often emphasized episodes of boys getting into trouble and praised only boys who had died, shows like *X Factor* and *Britain's Got Talent* presented teenage boys as regular people with interesting skills, and sometimes as people of great abilities.

Many critics contend the entertainment industry not only affects how people—especially young people—think of themselves, it can influence how they behave. In 1997, the R.J. Reynolds Tobacco Company dropped its Joe Camel character logo after many years of controversy over whether or not the cartoon was intended to attract children to Camel cigarettes. Even without tobacco company dollars, children and adolescents internalize positive messages about smoking (and drinking alcohol and having sex) from the behavior of characters in movies and the actors and actresses who portray them. Rap music is blamed for a host of modern problems, from inciting violence to the sexual objectification of women and the academic achievement gap among urban and black teenagers. Seemingly harmless music videos, such as the Top 40 selections that play on various television channels and online, are criticized for reducing attention spans and suggesting to teenagers that all information ought to be presented in short, flashy segments, to the bane of educators everywhere. More than one journalist has loudly opined that young people are ruining Western civilization, and that the entertainment industry has made them do it.

Such blanket statements may seem unfair compared to the volume of positive behaviors actively promoted by organizations and individuals in the entertainment industry. Political organizations often align with celebrities to attract young voters' attention to important causes; in 1992, Rock the Vote increased youth voter turnout by 20 percent, reversing a twenty-year trend. Actors and musicians speak earnestly in public service announcements, extolling the virtues of the local library, staying off drugs, wearing seat belts, avoiding disease, recycling, and reporting bullies. Many entertainers take the next step and found or fund charities and nonprofit groups specifically to support children and adolescents, such as Shakira's Pies Descalzos Foundation to establish and fund schools in impoverished regions of Colombia, and the Jonas Brothers' Change for the Children Foundation, which promotes youth volunteerism, diabetes awareness, and the Special Olympics.

The following chapter investigates some of the ways that the entertainment industry transmits cultural, social, and behavioral messages to children and adolescents, and examines how children and adolescents respond to such stimuli, as individuals and as a group.

> *"Children's television programmers . . .*
> *are leveraging the strength of their*
> *brands to address the issue through new*
> *programming, products, and licensing*
> *agreements to encourage activity and*
> *good nutrition."*

Super-Sized Kids: Obesity, Children, Moral Panic, and the Media

Rebecca Herr Stephenson and Sarah Banet-Weiser

Dr. Rebecca Herr Stephenson is a postdoctoral researcher at the University of California, Irvine; Dr. Sarah Banet-Weiser is an associate professor in the Annenberg School for Communication & Journalism at the University of Southern California. The following viewpoint appeared as a chapter in the book, The Children's Television Community, *an anthology of essays that analyze the organizations, major players, and approaches to children's programming, in addition to exploring its history and speculating about its future. The authors of this viewpoint argue that blaming television for childhood obesity is just hysteria and credit children's television programmers for promoting healthy lifestyles to kids.*

As you read, consider the following questions:

1. According to the authors, what corporate and commercial activities constitute the phenomenon of "social marketing"?

2. How does using popular cartoon characters, such as SpongeBob SquarePants, to promote healthy eating send conflicting messages to children, according to the authors?

3. As stated by the authors, what are the components of Sesame Workshop's Healthy Habits for Life program?

In the last few years, there has been an increasingly sensationalized public discourse about the "epidemic" of childhood obesity in the United States. Recent headlines point to the seriousness of the problem ranging from "Parents Might Outlive Obese Children" to "Fat Kids 'May Be Eating Away to Early Death.'" Reports about the future ill health of obese kids has led to a general hysteria over what the future will bring and the threat of high-profile obesity lawsuits has caused food companies to think hard about liability and public scrutiny. Together, these concerns have fueled the emergence of a moral panic about childhood obesity and have pointed to the media (television in particular) as the primary culprits corrupting children's bodies.

This latest moral panic draws upon a dichotomous understanding of children as *either* innocent victims of media influence *or* savvy media users. Those who blame television for the childhood obesity epidemic clearly adhere to the idea of children as innocent victims, and have proposed increased regulation of content and advertising as the solution to the problem.

Simultaneously, under pressure to do something to address this moral panic, children's media companies have undertaken several initial efforts to combat childhood obesity and mold their young viewers into morally and physically virtuous citizens, indicating their embrace of the idea of children as savvy media users. . . .

The War on Fat

Childhood obesity is the most recent in a long history of moral panics in the United States about the role of media use in the health and well-being of children. Reports from the Centers for Disease Control [and Prevention], the [Henry J.] Kaiser Family Foundation, the American Academy of Pediatrics, and others, have argued that this latest "epidemic" to hit the United States is connected to both the amount of time that children sit in front of television sets and to the content of television advertisements geared toward children. Such studies have prompted parents, educators, and media advocates to demand the FCC's [Federal Communications Commission's] attention to the issue.

Although the FCC has not yet imposed new regulations, cable and broadcast networks have moved quickly to quell this recent panic in ways that prove to be profitable. Using a kind of "social marketing" strategy similar to the antismoking campaigns developed by Philip Morris, Inc., some television networks have created not only new programming and public service announcements [PSAs], but also have joined in "strategic alliances" with food corporations such as Kraft and McDonald's. Such strategic alliances allow corporations to diffuse public panic about the nation's unhealthy children while simultaneously keeping those same children in front of the television and eating fast food. McDonald's and Burger King are now offering fruit and milk alongside of soda and fries, and children's television programmers such as Sesame Workshop, the Disney Channel, and Nickelodeon [Nick] are leveraging the strength of their brands to address the issue through new programming, products, and licensing agreements to encourage activity and good nutrition without discouraging television viewing. . . .

The response of the children's media industry to the childhood obesity "crisis" thus far has comprised an interesting conflation of the commercial marketing practice of branding and social marketing. For the children's television industry, adding concern for fitness and nutrition to the network brand is both an effective way to connect with viewers (and their panicked parents) and an essential weapon in deflecting the blame placed on television for the increase in childhood obesity. However, because the industry's profits are, in part, based on viewers eating branded snacks while viewing, promoting activity and healthy food can be a dangerous undertaking. For now, the benefits of including healthy habits in network brands seem to outweigh the drawbacks, as the new focus has helped to encourage further brand loyalty in both viewing and purchasing habits. In addition, it has opened up opportunities to expand product lines with healthy snacks and branded equipment for kids' new, active lives.

Examples of social marketing (or entertainment education, as it is sometimes called) can be seen in the increase of programs and PSAs encouraging healthy eating and activity habits. Through social marketing, topical information is woven into the story of a program, modeling behaviors and providing factual information about the desired behavior. For example, an episode of Disney's pre-teen comedy *That's So Raven* titled "Food for Thought" addressed concerns about the presence of fast-food outlets in school cafeterias, a prevalent practice in schools across the country. In this episode, a student organizes her peers to protest the renovation of the school cafeteria into a fast-food court. Similarly, an episode of *The Simpsons*, titled "The Heartbroke Kid," questioned the practice of vending machine contracts in schools. The potential for weight gain and resultant health problems is (in typical *Simpsons* style) exaggerated and satirized through Bart's experience consuming a diet of vending machine treats. Although the positive effects of social marketing have been noted for a variety of social and health-related topics, the technique provides limited long-term attention to the issue. In order to have real "sticking power" in the minds of young viewers and consumers, the message must become an integral part of the network brand.

The VERB Campaign

The VERB campaign created and executed by the Centers for Disease Control and Prevention (CDC) is an example of the merging of social marketing and branding. According to the program's Web site, VERB's objective is to "encourage[s] young people ages 9–13 (tweens) years to be physically active every day." The campaign is entering its second phase and expanding its reach through additional advertising and marketing in the form of PSAs, printed ads, and regularly scheduled events in conjunction with community organizations such as the National Recreation and Park Association. The campaign has been deliberately constructed in a way that utilizes corporate branding strategies. Careful design of the messages, media products, and events have led to the establishment of VERB as "multicultural, inspirational, motivational and a source of great ideas for activities that get tweens' bodies moving." The use of humor and sarcasm, appealing visuals, popular music, and celebrity involvement have contributed to the "cool factor" of the campaign.

In addition to its own branding, VERB has established strong relationships with several children's media companies including Disney, Kids WB, and Nickelodeon. Each of these networks air customized PSAs featuring the network's characters. In addition, VERB sponsors events in conjunction with these networks such as Nickelodeon's Worldwide Day of Play.

There is a synergistic relationship between the VERB brand and the network brands, which provides the opportunity for both parties to extend and shape their brands in a positive way. Through the mutual constitution of the brands, VERB increases its reputation as cool, hip, and part of the tween culture while the network brands incorporate activity and efforts to reduce childhood obesity.

Nickelodeon has made several additional efforts to incorporate healthy habits into the network brand. For example, the network has created "Nicktrition," a series of health and wellness suggestions for children and parents, to assist in rebranding existing food products to be consistent with its new dedication to health and fitness. Nicktrition tips, which range from control of portion sizes to encouraging family activity, appear on the packaging of many Nickelodeon-branded products, from *Dora the Explorer* fruit snacks to *SpongeBob SquarePants* Pop-Tarts. Although the intentions behind "Nicktrition" are good, the campaign has been criticized for presenting young consumers with conflicting messages—as labels advising kids to drink water and eat vegetables on the back of boxes of macaroni and cheese are bound to do. Recent licensing agreements with Boskovich Farms, Grimmway Enterprises, and LGS Specialty Sales will allow Dora, SpongeBob, and characters from Nick's new program *LazyTown* to appear on bags of spinach, carrots, and fruit. These agreements are also well-intentioned steps in the right direction, but open the network up to criticism for using the same characters to advertise processed junk food and produce at the same time.

The Networks' Efforts to Educate Children

Nickelodeon has also emphasized support for physical activity in its brand. The network's Worldwide Day of Play and Let's Just Play initiatives encourage viewers to turn off the television in favor of active play. Let's Just Play is a long-term effort that was begun in 2003 to encourage and "celebrate active,

One Network's Message to Parents

In our program, we've been making sure that we are eating lots of nutritious foods that are low in sugar, fat, and salt.

We call these healthy foods "anytime foods" because we can eat them every day. We've also been learning that foods like cookies, chips, sodas, and other snacks that are high in sugar, fat, and salt are called "sometime foods" because we should only eat them once in awhile.

You can help at home! Children need healthy options in order to make healthy choices. At home, give children lots of healthy foods and drinks to choose from so that no matter what they pick, you'll know they are getting the nutrients they need to grow and learn every day ("Would you like an apple or a banana? Would you like some salad or some yogurt?"). You can empower children as they make their own choices.

ANYTIME foods and SOMETIME foods Take a tour around the kitchen together and look at the foods you are eating every day to make sure you have lots of the anytime foods such as fruits, vegetables, whole grains, low-fat milk/cheese/yogurt, and lean meats. If you discover any chips, cookies, candy, sodas, or sports drinks, pause to remember that these foods are high in sugar, fat, and/or salt and are only sometime foods.

Sesame Workshop, "Making the Healthy Choice,"
Healthy Habits for Life Binder, *2007.*

physical play" for the fun and health of it. The initiative includes PSAs, grants for schools and community organizations to implement activity programs, and events sponsored by the network with its partners, the Boys & Girls Clubs of America and the National PTA [Parent Teacher Association]. The Worldwide Day of Play is one such event. In October 2004, Nickelodeon went off the air for the first time in its 25-year history, showing instead three hours of graphics encouraging families to go outside and play. This programming decision, like the decision to encourage healthy eating and exercise, is antagonistic to the network's larger mission. However, the Worldwide Day of Play, now a national event, has become a key part of Nickelodeon's identity as a network concerned with child health. Although Nickelodeon and other networks are encouraging their viewers to turn off the television, the concern with viewer well-being ensures that when viewers return to the couch, they will resume watching that network's offerings.

This new brand identity extends to program offerings. Nickelodeon's show *LazyTown*, an import from Iceland, is "designed to give kids the power to go play, move, dance, sing, make new choices and feel really good about it." The show's archetypical characters such as the hero Sportacus, a super-fit superhero, and Robbie Rotten, described as "the world's laziest super-villian" enact a 21st century morality play for viewers. Disney's preschool program *JoJo's Circus* also has its mission encouraging activity in its young viewers. *JoJo's Circus* is described as "TV's first movement-focused series ... designed to engage young children in activities that develop posture, balance, coordination, movement and spatial orientation, and build familiarity with exercise." In addition, Disney's preschool program, *Breakfast with Bear*, focuses on healthy habits including nutrition, hygiene, and activity. In this program, the character Bear (from *Bear in the Big Blue House*) will visit childrens' homes throughout the country to observe and participate in their daily morning routines.

Despite its history as a noncommercial network, PBS is also using commercial branding techniques to incorporate activity and nutrition into its preschool lineup. For example, in the summer of 2005, PBS premiered Happy Healthy Summer, a programming block highlighting PBS Kids programs that address healthy habits, including nutrition, exercise, rest, and hygiene. At the center of this effort is Sesame Workshop's Healthy Habits for Life initiative, which shapes content for *Sesame Street*'s curriculum as well as online resources at the Workshop's Web page and a growing group of related DVDs and other products. Segments focusing on healthy habits such as exercise, healthy eating, and the importance of a good night's rest are included in each episode. In addition, new characters related to healthy habits are slated for appearances in upcoming episodes. These long-term changes to the curriculum of the show reflect the incorporation of health consciousness into the Sesame Workshop brand. Perhaps the most poignant signifier of this change in the brand is Cookie Monster's new policy on cookie consumption—moderation.

The examples just noted are just a handful of the industry responses to the moral panic over childhood obesity. In addition to the networks mentioned, many independent production companies have produced videos, Web sites, and other interactive media that utilize social marketing to deliver messages about childhood obesity. Undoubtedly, such products will continue to appear in the marketplace until the panic is declared "solved." Until that time, the conflation of social marketing and commercial marketing/branding will continue to merge at the junction of the network brand. Nickelodeon will continue advertising its *SpongeBob SquarePants* spinach alongside *SpongeBob SquarePants* macaroni and cheese. Television advertisements and programs will continue to be used to discourage television viewing. Children raised with media brands will learn to associate healthy habits with their favorite networks and programs, and the actions of parents and networks will be reinforced by cultural understandings of children as innocent (yet media savvy) future citizens.

> *"Increased TV viewing in children and/or adolescents is associated with reduced fruit and vegetable consumption, more snacking, and increased intake of unhealthy and decreased intake of healthy foods."*

Beyond-Brand Effect of Television Food Advertisements on Food Choice in Children: The Effects of Weight Status

Jason C.G. Halford et al.

Dr. Jason Halford is a faculty member of the School of Psychology at the University of Liverpool. His research focuses on the psychological and biological factors that affect appetite and how they apply to the treatment of obesity and binge eating. He has published a variety of papers about the effects of television food advertising on children in a wide range of body weights. The experiment described in the following viewpoint suggests that not only do children tend to snack more after watching television

Jason C.G. Halford et al., "Beyond-Brand Effect of Television Food Advertisements on Food Choice in Children: The Effects of Weight Status," *Public Health Nutrition*, vol. 11, 2007, pp. 897–904. Copyright © Cambridge University Press 2007. Reprinted with the permission of Cambridge University Press and the author.

commercials for food, obese children are even more susceptible to advertisements for high-calorie snacks.

As you read, consider the following questions:

1. What percentage of advertisements during children's television programming in the United Kingdom is for food products, as stated in the viewpoint?

2. As described in the viewpoint, how did researchers test how children were influenced by food commercials?

3. How did the snack choices of obese children differ from the snack choices of children in other weight ranges?

The worldwide trend in childhood overweight and obesity is now a well-characterised phenomenon. Where national data are available, adiposity [body fat] has increased in both preschool and school-aged children in nearly every country studied. However, large variations in secular trends do appear across countries, and these relate to the degree of economic development and urbanisation. Increased availability of highly palatable, energy-dense convenience foods and increasing levels of sedentary activity may specifically contribute to rising rates of childhood obesity. Certainly, consumption of fast foods and soft drinks has risen markedly during the same period of time. Given the link between childhood obesity and adult ill health, how to mitigate these effects has now become an international health imperative.

Strong associations between the duration of daily television (TV) viewing and children's adiposity have been reported in numerous studies. Moreover, TV viewing behaviour predicts later adiposity, suggesting a causative role. While this relationship is in part mediated by exercise, much research has also demonstrated that TV viewing is also associated with specific differences in food intake and diet. Increased TV viewing in children and/or adolescents is associated with reduced fruit and vegetable consumption, more snacking, and increased intake of unhealthy and decreased intake of healthy foods. [Researchers] [Jan] Van den Bulck and [Jan] Van Mierlo found that every additional hour of TV viewed per day equated to an additional 653 kJ [kilojoule] consumed [~155 calories (cal)]. TV viewing is thus related both to the type and the amount of food consumed.

A link between TV viewing and obesity is clearly a concern, as TV viewing is a popular leisure-time pursuit for children across the globe. In the UK [United Kingdom], each week children watch an average of 17 hours of programming (both children's and family), a majority of which is commercial, i.e., broadcasting adverts [advertisements]. It has been shown that around half of the advertisements shown during children's programming in the UK are for food products, of which most are high in fat, sugar and/or salt, although new regulations regarding such advertising have recently been introduced in the UK. A recent US-based study estimated that between 27.2% and 36.4% of children's exposure to non-programme content was for food-related adverts. These were for cereals (27.6%), sweets (17.7%), snacks (12.2%), fast-food restaurants (12.0%) and beverages (8.8%). Numerous studies have shown that food adverts can alter children's preference for specific brands as the advertisers would intend. However, more recent data suggest they can also, under certain circumstances, increase energy intake.

Finding the Link Between TV and Obesity

A systematic review of the literature on the effects of advertising on consumption in children by [G.] Hastings et al. concluded that food promotion 'is having an effect, particularly on children's preferences, purchase behaviour and consumption'. The findings of the Hastings review would suggest that this form of brand promotion has clear effect beyond brand swapping, promoting a diet of energy-dense obesity-promoting foods. Certainly, it seems that children who watch more TV consume more of the most frequently advertised items, as well as less fruit, water and milk. Generally it is TV viewing and not advert exposure that has been linked to childhood obesity. However, in a recent cross-cultural study, which included data from the USA, Australia and eight European countries, a significant association between advert exposure and childhood obesity has been demonstrated. Specifically, a clear association between the prevalence of childhood obesity and the number of adverts for sweet and/or fatty foods advertised per 20-hour period of child-specific programming was found. It would seem logical then to infer that increased occurrence of obesity is caused by increased exposure to adverts promoting foods high in sugar and/or fat during viewing. . . .

In our previous study, the ability to correctly recognise food adverts was significantly associated with higher food intake following food advert exposure. It was also found that obese children recognised a greater number, and a greater proportion, of TV food adverts compared with non-food TV adverts. They also recognised more TV food adverts than the normal-weight children. In our previous study we tested advert recognition prior to food intake. However, this cognitive task may have affected children's food intake, either by distracting them from the effects of the food adverts or by acting as food stimuli themselves. Therefore, in the present study, food intake measurements were not preceded by the recognition task.

It was hypothesised that: (1) food advert exposure would increase food intake and alter food preferences in children; (2) these effects would be more pronounced in the overweight and obese children; and (3) food advert recognition would be related to children's weight status.

The Experiment

Fifty-nine children (32 male, 27 female) aged between 9 years 6 months and 11 years 2 months (mean 10 years 2 months)

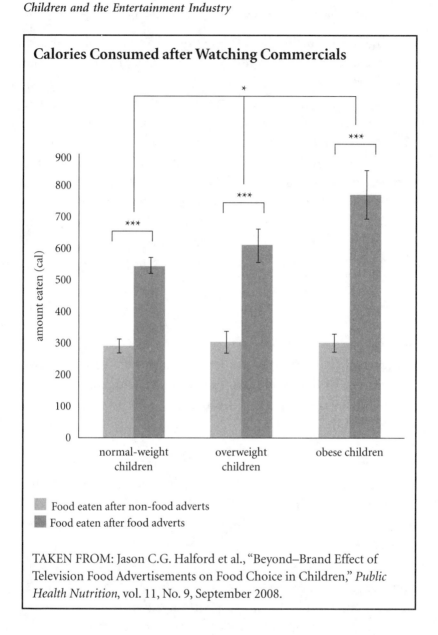

Calories Consumed after Watching Commercials

TAKEN FROM: Jason C.G. Halford et al., "Beyond–Brand Effect of Television Food Advertisements on Food Choice in Children," *Public Health Nutrition*, vol. 11, No. 9, September 2008.

were recruited from two classes of a UK school to participate in the study. This was an opportunity sample, no child or parent refused to participate; therefore the children were entirely representative of the two classes. In this study no children dropped out due to illness or for any other reason. . . .

Three videos were used, containing a collection of 10 non-food related adverts, a collection of 10 food-related adverts, and a cartoon. Advertisements were recorded from children's and family programming. . . . Each advert was approximately 30 seconds in length, for a total advert exposure time in both conditions of five minutes. These adverts were immediately followed by a 10-minute cartoon; the same cartoon was used in both conditions.

The children were given the opportunity to select and eat from an assortment of foods. The foods offered were: Quaker Snack-a-Jacks (cheese flavour); Haribo jelly sweets; Cadbury's chocolate buttons; Walkers potato crisps [chips] (ready salted flavour); and fruit (green seedless grapes). Each food item was chosen to represent a specific food category: low-fat savoury, low-fat sweet, high-fat sweet, high-fat savoury and low-energy density. . . .

Two weeks prior to the study, the children were asked if they wished to take part and consent forms were given to their parents.

On each occasion, the children were told that they would be viewing adverts followed by a cartoon. After viewing, the children were divided into groups of four or five. Each child was then presented with five plates, containing one of each of the five foods in either a standard portion size or 50 g [gram] weight, whichever was the greater. The children were instructed that they could eat as little or as much food as they liked, and were asked not to eat from one another's plates. The children were also told that if they finished the portion of a particular food, more of that food would be provided if they wished. A number of children did request extra food. There was no time constraint; however, neither session lasted beyond 20 minutes. Once the children had finished eating, the remaining uneaten food was re-weighed. After the second session, weight and height measurements were taken individually, in private, with a member of school staff present at all times. . . .

How Body Weight Influences a Commercial's Power

As predicted, the effect of food advert exposure produced the greatest response in the obese children. The intake response in overweight children was also significantly greater than in the normal-weight children. This is the first clear between-weight-status effect on intake in response to food advert exposure to be demonstrated in our studies. This may have been in part because of the greater proportion and total number of over-weight and obese children we were able to recruit to this study. Despite a smaller sample and lower proportional obesity, our previous research had found that BMI [body mass index] correlates with food advert recognition, suggesting that there was an underlying difference in the impact food adverts had on children of differing weight status, hence the rationale for this study. However, in the previous study, food advert exposure produced equivalent increases in food intake in all children irrespective of their weight status. In fact, in the previous study, trends for weight status differences in overall food intake were apparent in both control (toy advert) and food advert conditions. In contrast, in the present study no weight status differences in total food intake in the control (toy advert) condition were apparent.

Critically, these data provide the first clear definitive picture of an exaggerated intake response to food advert exposure based on weight status. In response to the food adverts, the obese children increased their intake by 471 cal from the control (toy advert) condition, compared with 306 cal in the overweight and 250 cal in the normal-weight children. The increase in intake in the overweight group was primarily driven by an increase in the intake of jelly sweets (143 cal) and chocolate (114 cal). Similarly, the increase in intake in the obese children was primarily driven by an increase in chocolate consumption (245 cal). This suggests that it is the effect of food advert exposure on the intake of sweet, energy-dense foods which differentiates the weight status groups. Moreover, in the food advert condition, total energy intake and intake of all the high-energy-density foods (jelly sweets, chocolate and crisps) were significantly and positively correlated with the children's standardised BMI scores.

Given that TV viewing is associated with current adiposity and predicts future weight gain, we believe that obese and overweight children may request more foods merely because of increased advert exposure. Certainly a direct association between TV advertisement exposure and obesity has recently been demonstrated. . . .

Caution must be taken when generalising the results of small-scale experimental studies to real-world behaviour. However, these data provide clear evidence of weight status differences, both in terms of total energy intake and in food choice, in response to food advert exposure, differences that were not apparent from our previous work. Moreover, they again demonstrate the statistically significant effect of advert exposure on children's food choice and total energy intake. These factors may well be critical in explaining the link between TV viewing, advert exposure and childhood obesity.

> "Picture books meant to acquaint young readers with nontraditional lives continue to crop up, making gay and lesbian topics increasingly prominent in mainstream children's publishing."

Children's Books Can Present a Diversity of Roles for Male and Female Characters

Nathalie op de Beeck

Nathalie op de Beeck is an assistant professor of English at Illinois State University and a frequent contributor to Publishers Weekly. *In the following viewpoint, she discusses the rise in gay/ lesbian gender roles in children's literature. While the stories have caused controversy among conservatives, they present diverse male and female character roles to children and allow a nontraditional view of family life.*

As you read, consider the following questions:

1. In what ways do the *King & King* books defy traditional gender stereotypes, according to the author?

2. According to the viewpoint, what stereotypes can arise from books such as *Molly's Family*?

3. What three children's television shows have brought controversy in the media, in which episodes have focused attention on gay/lesbian and nontraditional families?

According to the fairy tale, every handsome prince wants a princess—until Prince Bertie comes along. "I've never cared much for princesses," the lonely prince admits, to the consternation of his grouchy and marriage-minded mother. This prince just doesn't like girls, and he dismisses a series of them until, one day, his heart is stirred: not by Princess Madeleine who has come calling, but by her brother, Prince Lee.

Linda de Haan and Stern Nijland's exuberant picture book, *King & King*, is among the first mentioned by booksellers when asked about a current book for kids with a gay or lesbian spin. Published by Tricycle Press three years ago [2002], the book was followed by a sequel in 2004, *King & King & Family*, which describes the royal pair's tropical honeymoon and their adoption of a daughter. Happily ever after, it seems.

But for the people most interested in seeing gay and lesbian themes reflected in the mainstream culture—be it through books or television or film—there are still limitations. On the book side, demand outpaces the supply of relevant books, especially as gay and lesbian lifestyles approach greater acceptance. On the TV/film side, this acceptance is being resisted by no less a force than the U.S. secretary of education.

Growing Demand for Diverse Gender Roles

Elloyd Hansen, one of the owners of the Provincetown Bookshop in Provincetown, Mass., regularly sells the *King & King* books, especially during his town's well-attended gay family week every summer. "Hundreds of couples are here with families, so we do have a calling for it," he says.

Michael Cavanaugh, manager and buyer at Books of Wonder in New York City's predominantly gay Chelsea neighborhood, sees a real demand for gay- and lesbian-theme picture books, too, but he thinks good ones are in short supply. "We have a lot of requests, and there's definitely an interest," he says, having recommended *King & King & Family* to adoptive gay couples. But he is "hard-pressed to have in-depth discussion" about topical picture books because so few have impressed him.

Philip Rafshoon, owner and general manager of Outwrite Bookstore & Coffeehouse in Atlanta, agrees. "I see a growing demand, but I don't think it's being met," Rafshoon says.

It's not that there are no books out there for gay and lesbian parents and their children, or for nonconformist kids. Readers can find groundbreaking (if now dated) stories of children's gender ambiguity, like Charlotte Zolotow's *William's Doll* or Tomie dePaola's 1979 *Oliver Button Is a Sissy*; they can locate books on same-sex relationships and gay pride from Alyson Wonderland, the children's imprint of Alyson Publications. Alyson followed Lesléa Newman's much maligned but well-known classic *Heather Has Two Mommies* with stories of gay fathers, like Michael Willhoite's *Daddy's Roommate*, its sequel *Daddy's Wedding*, and Johnny Valentine's *One Dad, Two Dads, Brown Dad, Blue Dads*. Nonetheless, there remains "a big hole in the market," according to Linda Bubon, co-owner of Women & Children First bookstore in Chicago. Bubon believes that "the older books were published with the best intentions but not illustrated by real children's illustrators or written by people who understood the whole culture of children's literature. They can't compete with the beautiful artwork and lyrical writing of our best children's literature."

Although the pace is slow, picture books on gay and lesbian topics are gaining a foothold beyond the small independent houses like Alyson, and the scope of the titles is becoming more inclusive—or, perhaps, less exclusive.

Children's Stories with Nontraditional Roles

At Farrar, Straus and Giroux [FSG], executive editor Wes Adams—editor of Terence Blacker's middle-grade novel *Boy2Girl*—welcomes "books with a rebellious spirit. The longer I'm in [the publishing business]," he says, "the less patience I have with preachy, serious, sober titles. At this point, I'm looking for books with comic flair and an energetic approach to material."

In 2001, Adams signed author-illustrator Andrea U'Ren for *Pugdog*, an account of a female dog that rejects conventional feminine trappings. "As far as the gender issue behind it, my interest in that is the comedy of it all, the absurdity," Adams says. Similarly, *Heather* author Lesléa Newman questions gender roles in two new picture books, *A Fire Engine for Ruthie* (Clarion Books) and *The Boy Who Cried Fabulous* (Tricycle Press), although booksellers report mixed sales of Harvey Fierstein and Henry Cole's *The Sissy Duckling* (S&S [Simon & Schuster]).

Children's gender orientations remain tricky territory and still constitute a sub-subgenre of gay and lesbian publishing. Yet same-sex families are getting positive attention from mainstream publishing houses. Last year [2004], Adams's FSG colleague Margaret Ferguson worked with author Nancy Garden and watercolor illustrator Sharon Wooding on *Molly's Family*, the story of a kindergartner who comes under scrutiny from her classmates when she reveals that she has lesbian parents. Despite focusing on schoolroom discomfort in Molly, Garden insists that books for and about gay and lesbian audiences should not treat homosexuality as a problem. "At a conference, I went to a panel of children who were asked to speak about this," Garden recalls, "and I remember a girl with gay or lesbian parents said, 'I wish there were books for us in which it wasn't an issue.'"

At her publishing and distribution company, Two Lives Publishing, Bobbie Combs has "gotten feedback that people don't want an 'issue' book anymore. They want books that normalize the family, about a child who just happens to have two [same-sex] parents. But there are still not too many of those," Combs says.

"What I think is so wanted is books that are about other stuff, and just happen to show a kid who has two moms so you're not addressing it as the issue," says Women & Children First's Bubon. She strongly recommends inclusive books like Susan Meyers's *Everywhere Babies* (Harcourt), illustrated by Marla Frazee. "It's extremely subtle," Bubon explains, and goes on to describe images of mixed-race families, a crowded urban street corner where two moms push a stroller and a Gymboree class where two men sit side by side. "I point it out to people who are looking for books that have real diversity," she says.

Picture books meant to acquaint young readers with nontraditional lives continue to crop up, making gay and lesbian topics increasingly prominent in mainstream children's publishing. The fact that some booksellers still see slim pickings underscores the challenges ahead. "All children deserve to see themselves reflected in their books," says Nicole Geiger, the publisher of Tricycle Press.

Diverse Character Roles Brew Controversy

While visual images of gay and lesbian families have grown easier to find in picture books, the topic has grown increasingly controversial in the media. Television, after all, is a more visible medium; its images are broadcast rather than confined to a book purchased by a family. On the little screen, characters like SpongeBob SquarePants have been criticized for extending messages of tolerance that implicitly include gay, lesbian and other nontraditional families. In 1999, the *Teletubbies'* androgynous Tinky Winky drew the Rev. Jerry Falwell's ire for carrying a red satchel and wearing an inverted purple triangle on his/her (its?) head, while the *Chicago Tribune* (Mar. 15, 2005) reported that Marshall Field's stood accused of a "hidden gay agenda" for its Snow White and the Seven Dwarfs display, which showed seven men cohabiting.

Marc Brown, creator of the popular PBS series *Arthur* and *Postcards from Buster*, became embroiled in just such a cartoon-related controversy in January [2005]. In an episode titled "Sugartime!" Buster (a third-grade rabbit) visits Vermont for the spring maple syrup harvest and stays with a family that includes a lesbian couple and their three mixed-race children. Throughout the segment, Buster reflects on what to get his own mom for Mother's Day, and the ordinary images of family life demystify the same-sex couples.

"Sugartime!" initially was slated to air February 2 [2005]. But WGBH-TV in Boston, which produced the episode, came under scrutiny the day after Margaret Spellings began her tenure as U.S. secretary of education. Department of Education deputy press secretary Chad Colby remarked that PBS president Pat Mitchell "had reservations about the show before [Spellings's] comments. . . . The only thing that happened for the department is that the secretary sent the letter [to Mitchell, denouncing the show]. Everything else has been a reaction to that."

Brown said he was astonished by the letter. "The last person I expected to be censored by was the secretary of education," he said. "I was surprised that on practically the first day of her appointment she would go after *Postcards from Buster*."

Brown felt stung a second time when PBS agreed to pull the segment. In the weeks that followed, the nation's 349 public television stations decided individually whether to air "Sugartime!" absent Department of Education approval. As of this writing, 52 stations (representative of 54% of U.S. households) have aired or decided to air it.

At the moment, *Buster's* fate and funding remain in doubt. As Brown continues planning TV episodes, he says, "My formula is pretty simple: I look for ways to be helpful to children and families, to do things I learned from my good friend Fred Rogers. When all this started to happen, my first thought was, 'I wish I could call Fred,' because he had a wonderful way of going right to the heart of matters. What would Fred have said?"

> *"Most themes represented in children's books reflect the expectation that male characters will use their brains to effectively and creatively solve problems, while female characters are portrayed as more concerned with appearance."*

Most Children's Books Present Male and Female Characters in Traditional Gender Roles

Ya-Lun Tsao

Ya-Lun Tsao was a doctoral candidate at the College of Education at the Pennsylvania State University in 2008, when this article was published. The following viewpoint first appeared as an article in the journal Reading Improvement; *it presents summaries of many studies about the portrayals of males and females in books for children, particularly for younger children. The author argues that the casting of characters in traditional gender roles influences how children are socialized and can affect the beliefs they have about men and women's personalities and re-*

Ya-Lun Tsao, "Gender Issues in Young Children's Literature," *Reading Improvement*, vol. 45, Fall 2008, pp. 108–114. Copyright © 2008 by Project Innovation, Inc. Reproduced by permission.

sponsibilities in adulthood. The author further contends that books should be chosen by parents and educators to teach and promote gender diversity.

As you read, consider the following questions:

1. As stated by the author, what are some typical descriptions of male and female characters in children's books?

2. What social lessons do children's books teach to young readers, according to the author?

3. As explained by the author, what kinds of books should teachers of young children select for use in their classrooms and lesson plans?

The impact of gender-role stereotyping in children's literature has been examined in numerous studies over the past decades. Many researchers have acknowledged that literature can influence the gender stereotypes of young children, and that gender bias is present in the content, language, and illustrations of many children's books. In other words, children's books are an important cultural mechanism for teaching gender roles to children. The bias influencing gender stereotypical thinking may limit children's choices, interests, and abilities. In most children's picture books, males characteristically dominate titles, pictures, and texts. Female characters, on the other hand, are not only underrepresented in titles and central roles, but also appear unimportant. According to researchers' findings, 85% of the main characters in stories for children are male, and female characters rarely do anything. Examples of sexism are clearly abundant, even from a quick glance at a dozen randomly selected books.

Gender stereotypes in literature prevent female human potential from being realized by depriving girls of a range of strong, alternative role models. Moreover, present studies showed that female and male characters are not presented equally. Female characters were found to be presented significantly less often in pictures and titles than were male characters. Also consistent with gender stereotypes, male characters were more often described as potent, powerful, and more active than female characters.

As mentioned, gender bias is easily found in the content, language, and illustrations of a large number of children's books. This bias may be seen in the extent to which a main character represents a gender in children's books and how that gender is portrayed. Moreover, . . . contemporary society often categorizes both genders with outdated and stereotypical images and biased language, all of which are considered problems in children's literature.

According to [Masha Kabakow] Rudman [in the book, *Children's Literature*]:

> Books for children have reflected societal attitudes in limiting choices and maintaining discrimination. Most traditional books show females dressed in skirts or dresses, even when they are engaged in activities inappropriate for this sort of costume. Illustrations also have conventionally placed females in passive observer roles, while males have been pictured as active. Studies have demonstrated time and time again that illustrations confirm the subordinate, less-valued role for the female, while stressing the active, adventuresome, admirable role for male.

> In addition, most themes represented in children's books reflect the expectation that male characters will use their brains to effectively and creatively solve problems, while female characters are portrayed as more concerned with appearance. Females are depicted as dependent, emotional, silly, clumsy, and lacking intelligence. They are passive, gentle, domestic, motherly, and unassertive. Males typically are portrayed as competent and achievement-oriented, while the image of females is that they are limited in what they can do, and are less competent in their ability to accomplish things. That is to say, female characters are involved in few

of the activities and assigned few of the characteristics or goals that are accorded prestige and esteem in today's society. In reality, women do pursue and achieve goals, as well as engage in daily business/professional activities.

[Researchers] . . . asserted that gender development is a critical part of the earliest and most important learning experience of young children. Children's picture books not only possess an incomparable charm for children, but also have a long-term influence on their gender development. That is, in addition to entertainment, children's picture books also communicate cultural and social norms to young children. Illustrations also have an equal responsibility to tell the story because characters' pictures evoke feelings, emotions, and reactions as young readers observe illustrated facial expressions. Based on this affirmation of importance, children's picture books perform faithfully the role of furthering the development of children's gender identities.

Research Demonstrates Gender Inequalities

Much has been written about children's literature and gender stereotyping, describing its influences on the gender attitudes of children. Gender-role stereotypes affect how children perceive themselves. A negative portrayal of a child's own gender may affect that child's self-identity and self-esteem. Some researchers found that an awareness of stereotypes changed children's attitudes. Yet children who were read nonsexist stories over a sustained period of time reduced their notions of gender-role stereotypes. These children also developed fewer stereotypical attitudes about jobs after being read stories about people who fought gender discrimination.

According to findings . . . males predominated in situations with active mastery themes, such as cleverness and adventure, while females predominated in situations with "second-sex" themes, such as passivity and victimization. Also, females were greatly underrepresented in titles and central roles. Furthermore, the illustrations in children's picture books depicted most activity being accomplished by males. . . . This trend in children's books is based on the premise that "boys do, girls are," making gender stereotypes a strong influence affecting children's perceptions of the behaviors and attitudes of each gender. . . .

Recent studies on gender equality in children's literature found inequality in children's books. Although nonsexist books were more likely than sexist books to portray female characters who adopted male-stereotypical characteristics and roles, both types of books similarly portrayed the stereotypical female as a person devoted to domestic chores and leisure activities. Such portrayals may contribute to the perpetuation of gender inequality, particularly if touted as examples of equality.

Book Characters and Gender Perception

As mentioned earlier, some conclusions can be drawn. First, gender development is a critical part of the earliest and most important learning experiences. For young children, picture books are important because they provide role models for children in defining standards for feminine and masculine behavior. Next, gender stereotypes and sexism limit children's potential growth and development. Nonsexist books, on the other hand, produce positive changes in self-concept, attitudes, and behavior.

In other words, children's gender attitudes may be positively changed through the reading of appropriate children's literature and other book-related activities. Moreover . . . young children's attitudes, while still generally stereotypical, are beginning to be more flexible regarding occupational roles for men and women. They also suggested that a valuable resource for influencing children's gender attitudes is the careful selection of reading material and the use of books and related activities that promote gender-neutral attitudes. . . .

Grading Children's Television Shows

Name: _____   **Overall grade**
Network: _____
Genre: _____
Show description:

		Grade
Representation	Does the show use a balanced ratio of male and female characters?	
Appearance	How characters are portrayed in terms of their appearance. Does the show use color to identify gender and are broad ranges of features used to illustrate characters?	
Communication/ Interaction	How characters are portrayed in terms of their communication styles and interactions with other characters. Do they display characteristics such as assertiveness, confidence, sensitivity, kindness, adventurousness, etc.?	
Leadership & Independence	How characters are portrayed as leaders or followers. Do they act independently, initiate conversations and actions, show respect for others, etc.?	
Activities	How characters are portrayed in terms of their activities and physicality. Are characters portrayed doing only stereotypical activities (girls cheerleading and boys playing sports, for example) or are there a broad range of activities for each?	
Skills & Intelligence	How characters are portrayed in terms of their intelligence and abilities. Do they show aptitude with science, technology or math as well as art, dance or music?	
Comments:		

TAKEN FROM: TrueChild TV Report Cards, 2009. *www.truechild.org.*

Even books praised as nonsexist portrayed, at best, a narrow vision of gender equality in which women adopt stereotypically male attributes and roles. Most striking was the frequent portrayals of females in stereotypically common personalities, domestic roles, and leisure roles.

Nonsexist books succeeded in portraying female characters as adopting the characteristics and roles identified with masculine gender roles. However, they did not portray male characters as adopting aspects of feminine gender roles or female characters as shedding feminine gender roles. In addition, these findings support the conceptualization of sexism as a multidimensional construct. Even in the domain of children's literature, sexism manifests itself in diverse ways.

Children's reading materials are a widely available cultural resource that children may draw on to make sense of gender. Books for children have reflected societal attitudes in limiting choices and maintaining discrimination. Most picture books show females dressed in skirts or dresses, even when they are engaged in activities for which the costumes are inappropriate. Illustrations have conventionally placed females in passive observer roles, while males have been pictured as active. Illustrations confirm the subordinate, less-valued role of the female and stress the active, adventuresome, and admirable role of the male. When a female is permitted to retain active qualities, the message conveyed to children is that she is the notable exception because all other girls in books are "normal."

Children's picture books have an increasingly significant place in children's development because they offer young children a multitude of opportunities to gain information, to become familiar with the printed pictures, to be entertained, and to experience perspectives other than their own. Gender is perhaps the basic dimension through which children perceive their social world and their places in it. Gender shapes social organization, influences how young children interact with each other, and even determines how young children evaluate themselves. Over the past decades, increased female representation in titles, central roles, and pictures appears to indicate that more and more authors of children's books are aware of and sensitive to women's changing roles.

Teachers Can Make a Difference

In order to build a gender-equal literature learning environment, it is important to consider the attitudes of both authors and teachers when selecting children's books. Ideally, all children's books used in classrooms should have well-rounded male and female characters. That is to say, teachers should select books in which individuals have distinct personalities regardless of their genders. Characters' achievements should not be evaluated on the basis of gender, and females should not always be portrayed as weaker and more delicate than males. In addition, teachers may choose books that have countersexist attitudes embedded in them. For example, feminist texts can help children recognize gender-stereotypical messages. Also, combining traditional and nontraditional books can spark discussion of how genders are portrayed in different books that promote gender-neutral attitudes.

Teachers need to make a conscious effort to select books that reflect fairness to both genders. Since young children cannot yet make this choice, the responsibility must be the adults'. Moreover, increased effort is needed from publishers and authors to provide children with literature that more closely parallels the roles of males and females in contemporary society.

The growing literature on antibias in curricula and culturally inclusive pedagogy in the early years of education provides many examples of the ways that programs can provide powerful messages about gender roles. The use of picture books that portray nontraditional gender roles, including boys and men in nurturing or caregiving roles, as well as girls and women in active, leadership roles, provides an important contrast to the commonly popular cultural messages often seen and heard by very young children. Hence, the use of appropriate children's literature must be well-timed as children construct their views of human diversity.

"There is now a whole body of evidence that links fashion and media images directly to the health and well-being of the wider population of teenage girls".

Images in the Media Negatively Impact Adolescent Girls

Fiona Bawdon

Fiona Bawdon is a writer for New Statesman. *In the following viewpoint, Bawdon argues that viewing media images of women, in print and on television, sends the message that women should be thin, which can psychologically harm adolescent girls who are unable to achieve the highly idealized shape of models and actresses. Although the media's focus on thinness and dieting is only part of what contributes to an eating disorder, the impact of our "size zero" culture cannot be overestimated.*

As you read, consider the following questions:

1. In a study carried out by Girlguiding UK, reported in the viewpoint, what did more than half of sixteen- to twenty-five-year-olds say was the "most important thing"?

2. Why, according to the viewpoint, are adolescents the group most likely to suffer long-term ill effects from eating disorders?

3. Why can even critical coverage of celebrities being "too thin" be harmful to eating disorder sufferers, according to the viewpoint?

As London Fashion Week sashayed to a close on 20 September [2007], most of the media coverage was of the clothes, rather than the skeletal frames of the girls inside them. Yet the week coincided with the publication of recommendations from a controversial inquiry into the health of fashion models, set up after two Latin American models died from eating disorders, one after collapsing on the catwalk.

In her report, the chair of the Model Health Inquiry, Baroness Kingsmill, said she had found "startling" evidence of the vulnerability of models, who are at "high risk" of eating disorders. The inquiry heard evidence from an editor who said she'd sat through "innumerable shows where I have been unable to take in the clothes through shock at the emaciated frames of models". A writer said the fashion world was "numb", looking at models only as "clothes hangers" and "failing to see whether they are healthy or not". The inquiry made 14 recommendations to improve the working lives of models, including banning under-16s from the catwalk and introducing compulsory medical checks and a trade union.

The importance of the report, however, is not just that it reveals exploitation of young women in the fashion industry. There is now a whole body of evidence that links fashion and media images directly to the health and well-being of the wider population of teenage girls.

The Media's Importance to Teen Girls

In a study of 3,200 young women carried out in February this year [2007] by Girlguiding UK, over half of 16- to 25-year-olds said the media made them feel that "being pretty and thin" was the "most important thing". A quarter of girls aged between ten and 15 said the same. The most influential role models by far (cited by 95 per cent of girls) were Kate Moss and Victoria Beckham, both of whom are famously thin. In another study—*Sex, Drugs, Alcohol and Young People*, by the Independent Advisory Group on Sexual Health and HIV, published in June this year—nearly 30 per cent of 11-year-old girls expressed dissatisfaction with their body weight, and one in ten was on a diet. By age 15, 46 per cent of girls were unhappy with their weight, and a quarter of them were dieting.

Professionals working in this field are convinced that the number of teenage girls with an eating disorder is going up, and that sufferers are getting younger. The majority are aged 14–25, but girls as young as eight have been diagnosed. The last reliable survey into eating disorders across Britain dates back to 1990, but in Scotland, where new research was conducted in 2006, there had been a 40 per cent increase since 1990.

Teenage girls say they are influenced by pictures of impossibly skinny women, even when they don't want to be. At a recent conference in London about teenagers and the media, organised by the campaign group Women in Journalism, one teenager encapsulated the views of many of the 50 or so girls present, saying the fashion to be super-skinny made her "feel really ugly. I know it's really stupid but I still follow it. It makes me feel really insecure".

The Effects of "Size Zero" Culture

This young woman's experience is all too common, according to Professor Janet Treasure, director of the eating disorders unit at the South London and Maudsley NHS [Foundation] Trust, who has conducted research into the impact of the "size zero" culture. She says looking at pictures of thin women re-

What Messages Are Magazines Sending to Girls?

The number of teen-focused magazines has increased dramatically from five in 1990 to 19 in 2000, and most teens regularly read magazines. For example, one study found that 47% of 8- to 18-year-olds reported having read at least five minutes of a magazine the previous day, and 22% reported having read a magazine for 20 minutes or more the previous day; on average, 8- to 18-year-olds reported reading magazines 14 minutes a day.

Much of the research analyzing the sexual content of magazines focuses heavily on teen girls' and women's magazines. One of the dominant themes about sexuality reported across these studies and across magazines is that presenting oneself as sexually desirable and thereby gaining the attention of men is and should be the focal goal for women. Girls and young women are repeatedly encouraged to look and dress in specific ways to look sexy for men, a phenomenon labeled "costuming for seduction," and to use certain products in order to be more attractive to and desired by males.

American Psychological Association,
Report of the APA Task Force on the Sexualization of Girls,
2007. www.apa.org.

duces self-esteem—and adolescents are among the most susceptible to these pressures. Adolescents are also the group most likely to suffer long-term ill effects from eating disorders because their bodies are still developing.

Susan Ringwood, chief executive of Beat, the eating disorders charity, gave evidence to the inquiry. She supports its conclusions, but says restricting its remit to protecting young women in the modelling industry, rather than tackling the impact of "size zero" culture on the wider population, was an opportunity missed.

Ringwood accepts that it's a gross oversimplification to blame the rise in eating disorders entirely on the media's focus on thinness and dieting, but says it does play a part. "Eating disorder sufferers say: 'How come it's OK for celebrities to look like that and not me? How come they're being celebrated on the front of a magazine and I'm in hospital being told I'm going to die?'"

Although the Model Health Inquiry acknowledged this is an area outside its remit, it included a recommendation for a code of conduct to govern the digital manipulation of photos. The inquiry heard evidence of retouching to make models look thinner or even to make ill models look well—something of great concern to those working with eating disorder sufferers. "These processes add pressure to models to meet an unattainable ideal," it said. One suggestion was for retouched photos to carry a "health warning" so that the reader knows what she's looking at isn't real. The teenagers at the London conference were previously unaware that magazine images are routinely airbrushed: thighs slimmed, wrinkles smoothed and blemishes removed.

Of course, media coverage of skinny women is far from universally positive. But even critical coverage of celebrities who are deemed to be "too thin" can make matters worse for eating disorder sufferers, according to Ringwood. Low self-esteem is a recognised factor: Sufferers don't think they are worthy of taking up any space in the world, and shrink accordingly. Seeing bodies that look similar to theirs being pilloried and described as revolting reinforces their own lack of self-worth, she says.

Bodies Beautiful

Ringwood acknowledges that the causes of eating disorders are many and complex; they include factors such as genetic disposition and personality type, often compounded by traumatic events—for instance, bereavement or bullying. "But the final piece of the jigsaw is the social context," she says. Add the media, which celebrate impossibly skinny bodies over all other types, and numbers of sufferers are bound to increase. She would welcome a move for magazines to specify when images have been retouched.

It is a view shared by many of the sufferers themselves. Asked what was the one thing that would help prevent such conditions, most sufferers said it would be for the media to show more "real" bodies. They ranked this as more important than greater understanding from parents, or even greater medical knowledge. "Why can't the media promote healthy, normal-sized people?" lamented one typical respondent.

Ringwood says the media and the fashion industry should present a more diverse mix of body types as beautiful and acceptable. Such a change would not be a total solution by any means, but it would help, she argues. "We can't change brain chemistry and we can't protect young women from all forms of trauma. Of all the factors involved in eating disorders, images in the media are the one area we can change".

Periodical Bibliography

The following articles have been selected to supplement the diverse views presented in this chapter.

Diana Appleyard and Sadie Nicholas
"Meet the Pre-Teen Beauty Addicts," *Daily Mail*, August 7, 2007.

Jennifer L. Derenne and Eugene V. Beresin
"Body Image, Media, and Eating Disorders," *Academic Psychiatry*, May–June, 2006.

Janet M. Distefan, John P. Pierce, & Elizabeth A. Gilpin
"Do Favorite Movie Stars Influence Adolescent Smoking Initiation?" *American Journal of Public Health*, July 2004.

Jim Kavanagh
"Ad Council Gets Creative to Get Your Attention," CNN.com, September 3, 2009.

Joanna McCarthy
"Tobacco Firms Target China, Indonesia Youth," Australian Broadcasting Company, April 22, 2009.

Matt Painter, Zareena Asad, and David Holmes
"Teenage Boys and the Media: Report of Findings," Women in Journalism, March 2009. www.womeninjournalism.co.uk.

Nancy Signorielli
"Aging on Television: Messages Relating to Gender, Race, and Occupation in Prime Time," *Journal of Broadcasting & Electronic Media*, June 2004.

Freesia Singngam
"'SeeMore' Teaches Kids to Be Safe," *Daily Campus* (UConn), September 8, 2006.

Lindsey Tanner
"Pediatricians Blast Inappropriate Ads," Associated Press, December 4, 2006.

David Zurawik
"MTV Shows Harsh, Real World of Being 16 & Pregnant," *Baltimore Sun*, June 11, 2009.

OPPOSING
VIEWPOINTS®
SERIES

How Does the Entertainment Industry Engage Children?

Chapter Preface

When the Boston Public Health Commission (BPHC) designed its public awareness campaign for teenage sexual health, it turned directly to teenagers for help. In 2008 it announced the Get Reel: Check Yourself contest for teen-produced videos about sexually transmitted infections and safe sex. The winning submission was turned into an ad for the local Boston television channel, as well as FX, BET, and MTV. But BPHC didn't stop there; it also posted the video on YouTube and set up the Facebook group page, "sexED in Boston," in order to provide a community forum to make announcements and answer group members' questions about sex, disease, and other health topics. The BPHC hopes that by appealing to and directly involving teenagers in the spread of public health information—particularly at the social networking sites they frequent—they can reach more teenagers who will listen to their messages. The program is too new to calculate results yet, but within three months of its creation the Facebook group could count more than 1,500 "fans." Clearly, many adolescents are tuning in.

It's no marketing secret that people pay attention to information that comes from people who resemble them. Advertisers go to great lengths to conduct studies about target demographics and study the responses of test audiences to ad campaigns that best match them. It is why female actresses promote lipstick in commercials on women's cable channels, male actors talk about electric razors during radio sports broadcasts, and kids are pictured on the front of the Connect Four game box in the toy aisle. Because teenagers are spending more and more of their free time on social networking Web sites and sending text messages to each other, marketers are following them there.

This trend, like all trends, has benefits and drawbacks. On the one hand, being able to successfully navigate teens' media haunts (from online communities to teen-oriented cable channels) means getting their attention when it is important—such as when you have to deliver information about sexual health. On the other hand, using teens' social and entertainment outlets to deliver messages muddies the content and the environments: Information that appears disguised as entertainment or social interaction lessens in importance; and entertainment sites that are flooded with commercial, moral, or educational messages will lose their audience. Think again about the Boston Public Health Commission. It has established a presence on a social networking site but it does not pretend to be anything but an educational group. In fact, the word "Ed" appears in its name on Facebook. Teens already hanging out on the site know right away what to expect from this group—it is a friendly place that does not pretend to be a friend. Contrast that to people on Facebook who present themselves as individuals to befriend, only to start promoting commercial or educational interests. Most teens can readily discern when a "friend" is really a promotional message in disguise, and they soon cut off such relationships for good.

Young children, however, are not so savvy. Despite being adept at finding teen programming on television and logging on to their own profiles on social networking sites, they are still developing the critical thinking skills that adolescents use to distinguish blatant marketing from real entertainment or friendly relationships. They are much more vulnerable to promotional material that crosses media platforms, and confuse commercial interests with personal interests. Health and educational organizations take advantage of this dichotomy and work with children's television developers to teach important lessons, such as the value of reading or regular exercise, in popular children's television shows. This influence also carries over to other programs and entertainment, because children trust these characters to teach them how to behave. Disney Channel's Handy Manny stresses to children the value of teamwork on his television show, and then waves at them from the front of the Kern's fruit juice carton at the grocery store, telling them what to drink, too.

The following chapter investigates some of the ways in which the entertainment industry engages the attention of young children and adolescents, how youth audiences interact with many types of media, and how target audiences are defined and quantified.

> "61 percent of American children under two watch TV or videos, and 43 percent watch every day."

Entertainment for Babies and Toddlers Is a Growing Industry

Janine DeFao

Janine DeFao is an associate editor at Bay Area Parent, *a weekly newsletter affiliated with the Parenthood.com Web site. Previous to this position, she was a reporter for the* San Francisco Chronicle, *the largest newspaper in Northern California, for which she wrote the following viewpoint about the launch of the BabyFirstTV subscription cable network. BabyFirstTV, available internationally, advertises that it has been designed by educational experts and that it inspires young children's developmental skills. DeFao notes that while some critics debate whether television can teach babies developmental skills, others debate whether babies should watch television at all. Regardless, she states, the channel is popular with parents.*

As you read, consider the following questions:

1. As described by the author, what kinds of programming is shown on BabyFirstTV?

2. What recommendations has the American Academy of Pediatrics made regarding the amount of television small children should watch, as cited by DeFao?

3. According to DeFao, what false claims has BabyFirstTV been accused of making?

In an era of increasing niche programming on TV, women have the Oxygen network, men have Spike TV and some pets are even agog at Animal Planet.

Now, infants can pull up a bouncy chair, grab a bottle and have round-the-clock access to the nation's first channel for babies, BabyFirstTV, featuring three-minute segments designed for babies as young as six months.

The satellite channel, which debuted on Mother's Day [in 2006], touts itself as a "learning experience" for babies and their parents with developmental benefits. But it has come under fire from child development experts who say the claims are false and fly in the face of the American Academy of Pediatrics' recommendation of no TV at all for children under age two.

"I had that appalled, shocked reaction. (Babies) are these wide-open, defenseless, clueless targets," said Berkeley child psychologist Allen Kanner, cofounder of the national group Campaign for a Commercial-Free Childhood, which has filed a false advertising complaint against the channel with the Federal Trade Commission [FTC].

But some parents have had the opposite response. Kathy King, a Sacramento-area mother of two, signed up after coming across a free trial.

"They were both mesmerized," the middle school science teacher said of her sons, two-year-old Wyatt and ten-month-old Wesley.

Hardly the First of Its Kind

BabyFirstTV is not alone. Early entrants into the market nearly a decade ago included the *Teletubbies* TV show from Britain, geared for one- and two-year-olds, and Baby Einstein, which sells DVDs for children as young as one month. PBS last year launched a 24-hour cable channel called Sprout for two- to five-year-olds. And Sesame Workshop, the nonprofit organization behind *Sesame Street*, this spring released "Sesame Beginnings," DVDs for the under-two crowd.

"Is it right for them to be watching? The fact of life is, they are watching," said BabyFirstTV cofounder Sharon Rechter. "Parents should watch with them appropriate programming they can enjoy."

Rechter, 31, now pregnant with her first child, said she started the satellite channel—available on DISH Network and DIRECTV for $10 a month—when she saw a "great need" as her friends had babies. She estimated the market for children's DVDs and videos at $1.5 billion.

The commercial-free channel offers 44 series, including original programming and segments from top-selling videos such as Brainy Baby.

They range from a show that teaches sign language to a cartoon duck who guesses animal sounds to a black train chugging across a white background while classical music plays.

Rechter declined to release subscription figures for Baby-FirstTV but said the Los Angeles company is meeting its business goals and plans to expand to cable next year. The company could not provide contact information for any Bay Area subscribers, but Rechter said California is one of its top markets.

Possible Benefits to Babies Who Watch

A [2006] study this spring by the Henry J. Kaiser Family Foundation in Menlo Park found that 61 percent of American children under two watch TV or videos, and 43 percent watch every day. Nineteen percent of children under one and 29 percent of children ages two to three had televisions in their own rooms.

The study found that many parents believe television is beneficial, even educational, for their children, despite the recommendation by the nation's pediatricians in 1999 that it remain off limits to children under two.

The small amount of research on television watching for young children is inconclusive.

A Sesame Workshop study showed a positive relationship between viewing *Sesame Street* and preschoolers' achievement in reading and math, though other research shows a negative correlation between achievement and TV, said Vicky Rideout, director of the Kaiser [Family] Foundation's Program for the Study of Entertainment Media and Health.

Rideout said many studies show that children learn better by doing than by watching. Some research has shown that children mimic both violent and "pro-social" behavior seen on TV, while other research links television with both obesity and attention problems, she said.

But "babies watching baby videos and DVDs is a huge unknown," she said.

"In essence, we're conducting a big experiment on this generation of kids before we know what the impact of these media are," Rideout said.

Is Watching Television Really Educational?

That's one reason the American Academy of Pediatrics has no plans to modify its recommendation that children under two engage in no "screen time" and that toddlers watch no more

The "Play-Time, Snack-Time, Tot-Time" Conference: Targeting Pre-Schoolers and Their Parents

A presentation by Paul Kurnit, president of Griffin Bacal, a leading ad agency specializing in the children's market, explored in detail the phenomenon of "KGOY (Kids Getting Older Younger)" and the subject of "New Media for the 0–3" age group [at a conference for leading advertising, marketing, and programming executives]. Conference participants listened to "research findings and case studies from people involved in brands such as Thomas the Tank Engine, Teletubbies, Carter's, Sesame Street, Elmo's World, and Weeboks," and heard a presentation on insights "into the motivations behind today's mom's behavior and how you, as marketers, can capitalize on these motivations."

Among the objectives of the conference were to: "review marketing practices that drive loyalty in the preschool market" and "analyze different research and focus group methods used in determining the wants and needs of a preschool child." One workshop provided "hands-on training" in the latest trend in effective toddler and youth research: anthropological research, and the use of "observational research techniques" to help marketers "find out the desires of toddler-age consumers," because "moms, dads, and grandparents are often unaware of what [young children] do and really need." These techniques, participants were told, allow them "to immerse [themselves] in the environment and learn the deep needs of the individuals being observed" and "to identify [children's] real needs and motivations" in order to "develop products that answer these desires."

The Motherhood Project, Watch Out for Children: A Mothers' Statement to Advertisers, *2001. www.motherhoodproject.org.*

than two hours of quality programming each day, said pediatrician Don Shifrin, who heads the group's communications committee.

"Children need to live in a three-dimensional world, not a two-dimensional world. They need interactions with caregivers, not a screen," said Shifrin, of Bellevue, Wash.

Products such as Baby Einstein and Brainy Baby DVDs have been successful in convincing parents they can give children an edge, despite the lack of evidence, Shifrin said.

BabyFirstTV bills itself as offering content "tailored to meet the needs of infants and children" through age three.

The channel color-codes its various programs in seven categories from "encouraging children to develop language" to engaging children in "identifying patterns of thinking."

And its original segments, both animated and live-action, contain subtitles to help parents interact with children while watching, such as, "Name all the colors you see, and encourage your child to repeat after you."

The channel encourages parents to watch with their children, though Kaiser's Rideout said her research has shown that most parents rely on TV for their children when they need do things like take a shower or cook dinner.

King, the teacher who lives in the Sacramento suburb of Orangevale, said she often will watch BabyFirstTV with her sons.

"But sometimes it's a little helpful when you're trying to clean the kitchen and need to say, 'Give Mommy five minutes,'" King said.

She is not concerned about the American Academy of Pediatrics' recommendation.

"I think it just comes down to parenting," she said. "If I thought it was detrimental to their brain development, they would not be watching."

False Claims?

The Campaign for a Commercial-Free Childhood, based in Boston, filed complaints in May and June with the Federal Trade Commission against BabyFirstTV, Baby Einstein and Brainy Baby, accusing them of making false and deceptive claims when they say their programs have educational and developmental benefits. It asked the FTC to prohibit the companies from making the claims and to require them to prominently display the pediatricians' warning.

Rechter downplayed the complaint against her company.

"I don't think we overpromise anything," she said.

One family that has no plans to tune in is Allen Kanner's.

His 21-month-old daughter, Cassidy Kanner-Gomes, doesn't watch any television or DVDs, yet Kanner still manages to take showers.

"She plays with toys or comes in and talks to me. I shower quickly," he said. "It hasn't been a big problem."

> *"'The time has come for a network that is exclusively dedicated to teenagers. . . .'"*

Entertainment for Teens Is a Growing Industry

PR Newswire

Started in 1954, PR Newswire *was established to send out text press releases to the media. Today,* PR Newswire *delivers multimedia content and news to investors, consumers, and the media. The following viewpoint discusses the launch of the first television network exclusively dedicated to teenagers. The trend of teen television has grown a great deal, and now the time has arrived for a teen-oriented television network.*

As you read, consider the following questions:

1. According to the article, what "gap" does VTV fill?

2. What "teen-created content" appears on VTV?

3. What age group does VTV target with their programming?

Celebrating today's youth and spirit, the world's first and only television network dedicated to teens, VTV:Varsity Television, was officially launched today on Galaxy 11, Transponder 13. VTV has now been added to Pod 14 of Comcast's Headend in the Sky (HITS), whose affiliates service nearly 7 million U.S. households. In addition, a letter of intent has been signed with the National Cable Television Cooperative, which has over 14.5 million basic subscribers.

VTV is set to capture one of the largest and most sought-after programming niches remaining in the television world. VTV fills the gap in youth programming between Nickelodeon (kids 3 to 12) and MTV (adults 18 to 34).

The new network is cofounded by Joe Shults, a member of the executive team that launched MTV, Nickelodeon and VH-1 as well as one of the original management members for E! Entertainment, and Kelly Hoffman, who brings more than two decades of financial and administrative experience in building start-ups into strong, profitable companies.

Appealing to Teenagers

"The time has come for a network that is exclusively dedicated to teenagers," said Shults, president. "This is a powerful, influential audience that deserves an entertainment channel all its own."

The 24-hour network includes teen-oriented series and films developed by the most respected producers and distributors in the world, as well as original videos and films created by teens themselves. The teen-created content includes student films, short-form animation, music videos, documentaries and teen-produced news broadcasts. Companies from which VTV has acquired programming include ABC International, CBC, CTV, Granada, RDF International, and Universal Television.

Credited with $170 billion in annual spending influence, teens are the largest consumers of music, motion picture productions, DVDs, personal electronics, snacks and soft drinks,

Teenagers Are Products, Too:
A Discussion with Bonnie Liedtke
of the William Morris Agency

Bonnie Liedtke: The concept of kids being brands is much more real now. When a client comes in, we also have to discuss digital areas, like Web sites, digital platforms, publishing and clothing lines. That's something I would have never thought of 15 years ago. We have an entire plan. Many different departments come into play. It's constantly changing.

[*Hollywood Reporter*:] Has that raised the expectations for young performers who want to be the next Miley Cyrus?

Liedtke: We're realistic. If there's not a clothing line that's interested in having a deal with the artist, then we tell them. But we can usually figure out the ones who are going to sell clothing in Target or do the Got Milk? campaigns.

Matt Belloni and Noela Hueso,
"Kid Gloves: The Exploding Youth Market Is
Changing the Way Young Actors' Careers Are Handled,"
Hollywood Reporter, *September 3, 2008.*

fast food, clothing and more. Advertisers seeking teens for their influence, high return on investment resulting from lifetime brand loyalty secured for consumer products during teen years, now have a targeted vehicle for reaching 13–18-year-olds with VTV.

"As the head of a large agency representing clients with strong youth brands such as Pepsi, Frito-Lay and Pizza Hut, we were constantly searching for an effective marketing platform to reach teenagers," said Bruce Orr, VTV's vice president of marketing and former CEO of TracyLocke. "With VTV, I believe they finally have that platform."

VTV has established relationships with high schools located in the top 100 television markets in the United States. These schools maintain professional caliber audio/visual equipment and production facilities that deliver compelling, high-quality content directly to VTV. Thousands of clips have been received to date with a growing number of new program submissions arriving weekly from hundreds of high schools and related youth organizations. This content is then edited and packaged into stand-alone vignettes that air several times an hour throughout the programming day.

VTV has built a loyal and active audience through its Web site. . . . VTV has been sneak previewed for the past two months, giving multiple system operator (MSO) executives and cable system operators a unique opportunity to view the network's 24-hour signal. As a result, VTV is currently in final distribution negotiations with some of the country's largest MSOs.

"I saw the beginnings of a phenomenon in the early days of MTV and there are so many parallels between early MTV and VTV," said Rod Allen, vice president of affiliate relations and former regional director for MTV. "The response from the cable television community has been overwhelming."

[Editor's note: This cable channel went off the air in 2009.]

> *"By moving a chunk of a child's early education to the living room, the show ... shift[s] learning into the home."*

Children's Entertainment Can Be Educational

Jesse Walker

Jesse Walker is managing editor of Reason. *In the following viewpoint, Walker details the beginnings of* Sesame Street *and the now popular combination of children's entertainment and education. Walker details the motivations for the foundation of a televised preschool, and follows* Sesame Street *through its history as it struggles to live up to the task. Whether or not one approves of televised education, Walker asserts, it is undeniable that* Sesame Street *changed the way the world views children's television.*

As you read, consider the following questions:

1. Name two types of specialists that helped develop *Sesame Street*, according to the viewpoint.

2. What was one of the controversies surrounding *Sesame Street*, as cited by Walker?

Jesse Walker, "The Way to *Sesame Street*: The Politics of Children's Television," *Reason*, November 2009, pp. 60–61. Copyright © 2009 by Reason Foundation, 3415 S. Sepulveda Blvd., Suite 400, Los Angeles, CA 90034. www.reason.com. Reproduced by permission.

3. Name a current television program that is founded on the notion that "children can learn from television," as mentioned by the author.

It's hard to fathom just how unusual *Sesame Street* must have seemed when it debuted 40 years ago this month [November 2009]. The children's TV show didn't just mix entertainment with education: It was a full-blown collaboration between commercial showmen and social engineers. On one hand you had a team of educators, experts in child development, and officials at the Carnegie [Foundation for the Advancement of Teaching] and [the] Ford [Foundation] ... trying to create a televised preschool. On the other hand you had veterans of projects ranging from *Captain Kangaroo* to *The Jimmy Dean Show*, including a gang of puppeteers best known for making strange and funny ads. The program itself reflected both an antipathy to commercialism and a fascination with commercials, which served not just as a source for its parodies but as a model for its programming.

Educational Entertainment

The show emerged from the same Great Society milieu that had produced the Head Start preschool program. That guaranteed it would be a magnet for controversy. In his 2006 book *Sesame Street and the Reform of Children's Television*, the historian Robert Morrow notes that preschool in the '60s was frequently framed as a project for the impoverished, who were presumed to suffer from "cultural deprivation." Not surprisingly, many poor people found this attitude haughty and highhanded. The middle class, meanwhile, often saw the home as "a haven to be protected from intrusions by educators as well as by television."

Sesame Street was a liberal project, not a radical one (though Will Lee, aka Mr. Hooper, had been blacklisted in the McCarthy era). When Joan Ganz Cooney wrote the first feasibility study for the show, she consciously set herself against the traditional nursery-school notion that a child should "self-select" his activities, "incidentally learning all that is intellectually appropriate to his age and stage." This, Cooney wrote, amounted to "ignoring the intellect of preschool children." For radical critics of American schooling, by contrast, free exploration was the best nourishment an intellect could receive. The education critic John Holt, later a leader of the home-schooling movement, argued in the *Atlantic Monthly* in 1971 that "*Sesame Street* still seems built on the idea that its job is to get children ready for school. Suppose it summoned up its courage, took a deep breath, and said, 'We *are* the school.' Suppose it asked itself, not how to help children get better at the task of pleasing first-grade teachers, but how to help them get better at the vastly more interesting and important task— which they are already good at—of learning from the world and people around them."

Sesame Street Controversy

Inevitably, there were culture war controversies. Feminists complained that one human character, Susan, was too much of a traditional homemaker; conservatives grumbled that another woman, Maria, was too feminist. Morrow quotes a leftist viewer's complaint that the "cat who lives in the garbage can should be out demonstrating and turning over every institution, even *Sesame Street*, to get out of it." More broadly, there were the anxieties that always attach themselves to a centralized medium beaming unvetted images and ideas into the home. Marie Winn, author of the TV-bashing book *The Plug-In Drug*, spoke for many Americans when she warned that the program was "promoting television viewing even among parents who might feel an instinctive resistance to plugging such young children in." Monica Sims, an official at the BBC, felt the show's attempts to mold children's behavior were a form of "indoctrination" with "authoritarian aims."

Yet *Sesame Street* was enormously popular, and, pace Sims, it had an anti-authoritarian side. When the program's entertainers were at odds with its social engineers, the entertainers frequently won. If *Sesame Street*'s board of academic advisers had its way, the show's people and puppets wouldn't have interacted at all. (It was inappropriate, they felt, to mix fantasy and reality.) For its first two decades on the air, writers and performers were usually free to follow their creative instincts; and fortunately, the show had some very creative writers and performers. Besides Jim Henson and his fellow Muppeteers, who had honed their talents in ads, industrial films, and commercial TV shows, there were the songwriters Joe Raposo and Jeff Moss, each a remarkable pop craftsman, plus an array of inventive filmmakers (including Henson, who had been making experimental shorts at the same time he was producing ads).

Learning by Watching TV

As a result, *Sesame Street* became a rarity: a government program popular enough to sustain itself. The show quickly earned enough money via merchandising to wean itself from the federal teat. Public broadcasters today react to any threat to their funding by raising the possibility that *Sesame Street* would be forced to fend for itself. But if there's anything on PBS that can cover its costs independently, it's *Sesame Street*.

In a curious way, the show may have ended up doing more to empower the home than to batter down its doors. By moving a chunk of a child's early education to the living room, the show threatened to accomplish unintentionally what John Holt hoped it would do on purpose: to undermine the power of the schools and shift learning into the home.

Today the barriers to starting a children's video franchise are far lower than they were in the '60s. You don't need to beg a network for a spot on a tightly limited schedule. You can get your start on a niche cable channel, or even just on home

"Mindless" Entertainment Is Anything But

We know from neuroscience that the brain has dedicated systems that respond to—and seek out—new challenges and experiences. We are a problem-solving species, and when we confront situations where information needs to be filled in, or where a puzzle needs to be untangled, our minds compulsively ruminate on the problem until we've figured it out.

Parents can sometimes be appalled at the hypnotic effect that television has on toddlers; they see their otherwise vibrant and active children gazing silently, mouth agape at the screen, and they assume the worst: The television is turning their child into a zombie. The same feeling arrives a few years later, when they see their grade-schoolers navigating through a video game world, oblivious to the reality that surrounds them. But these expressions are not signs of mental atrophy. They're signs of *focus*. The toddler's brain is constantly scouring the world for novel stimuli, precisely because exploring and understanding new things and experiences is what learning is all about. In a house where most of the objects haven't moved since yesterday, and no new people have appeared on the scene, the puppet show on the television screen is the most surprising thing in the child's environment, the stimuli most in need of scrutiny and explanation. And so the child locks in.

Steven Johnson,
Everything Bad Is Good for You.
New York: Riverhead Books, 2005, pp. 180–182.

video. *Barney* . . . (not the most inspiring example, I know) was a series of independently produced VHS tapes before it came to TV. More recently, parents have been plunking down dollars for the allegedly educational DVDs for infants released under the brand name Baby Einstein. Given their content— long takes, minimalist *mise-en-scène*, an absurdism so deadpan it seems narcoleptic—a more accurate label might be Baby Warhol.

You needn't like *Barney* or Baby Einstein to approve of the change they represent: a world where DVDs, the Internet, and digital video recorders have given parents an impressive amount of control, should they choose to exercise it, over the moving pictures young children consume. The available options span the ideological and pedagogical spectrums, but they all owe something to the show that did more than anything else to impart the idea that kids could learn by watching TV. In 1969 the acting director of Head Start reassured schools that *Sesame Street* would not be "a substitute for the classroom experience." Forty years later, it has helped unleash an army of substitutes onto the world.

> *"Kids across the country will be listening to the dynamic programming of BusRadio, providing advertisers with a unique and effective way to reach the highly sought-after teen and tween market."*

Children's Programming in an Educational Setting Is Controversial

Caroline E. Mayer

Caroline E. Mayer is the consumer reporter for the Washington Post, *where she covers a wide variety of issues, from marketing scams and misleading ads to credit card solicitations and product-safety concerns. The following viewpoint features a company that provides a private radio service for school buses. Mayer explains that BusRadio plays music, hosts contests, and runs public service announcements, but also runs advertising for a captive audience of children unable to leave or change the sta-*

*tion. Although some see the service as beneficial, keeping stu-
dents in their seats, she says, others feel the potential for harm
outweighs any benefits.*

As you read, consider the following questions:

1. As cited by Mayer, what is the proposed content of one
   hour of BusRadio programming?

2. According to Mayer, what are some controversial aspects
   of BusRadio programming?

3. What are some possible advantages of having BusRadio
   available for students to listen to, as described by the
   author?

Soon, schoolchildren may be singing new lyrics to the classic "Wheels on the Bus."

"The ads on the bus go on and on, on and on . . ."

BusRadio, a start-up company in Massachusetts, wants to
pipe into school buses around the country a private radio network that plays music, public service announcements, contests
and, of course, ads, aimed at kids as they travel to and from
school.

As BusRadio's Web site explains: "Every morning and every afternoon on their way to and from school, kids across the
country will be listening to the dynamic programming of Bus-
Radio, providing advertisers with a unique and effective way
to reach the highly sought-after teen and tween market."

BusRadio, the Web site adds, "will take targeted student
marketing to the next level." Marketers can advertise and
sponsor contests or provide a celebrity deejay (perhaps to
promote that next CD or movie). They can also use BusRadio's
Web site to conduct surveys and test songs, CD covers, packaging and ads.

According to its Web site, BusRadio plans to operate in
Massachusetts this fall [2006], broadcasting to more than

102,000 students. By September 2007 it plans to take its programs national, reaching a million students. On the Web site, BusRadio listed Hagerstown, Md., as one of the areas it plans to serve. However, Chris Carter, director of public school transportation for Washington County (which includes Hagerstown), said he had never heard of BusRadio.

BusRadio's Business Model

The company is the brainchild of Michael Yanoff and Steven Shulman, the same two executives who created Cover Concepts, a company that has provided schools with millions of free book covers—full of bold, colorful ads for Kellogg's, McDonald's, Calvin Klein, Nike and other major national advertisers. Now owned by comic-book king Marvel Entertainment, Cover Concepts says it reaches 30 million school-age children in 43,000 U.S. public schools, which receive no funding for distributing the products.

Shulman declined to discuss BusRadio's plans, saying in an e-mail that it is "a relatively new company in a start-up mode." He said the "planned launch is in September, and until that time we have [a] policy in place not to comment on our business plan."

According to the company's Web site, school buses will be equipped—free—with custom-designed equipment that will carry the company's proprietary programs. It is unclear whether the school systems will also be paid for broadcasting BusRadio. In an hour's broadcast, 44 minutes will be devoted to music and news, six minutes to public safety announcements, two to contests and eight to advertising. On most commercial radio stations, there is usually ten to 12 minutes, sometimes more, of advertising.

BusRadio says pilot tests have shown that students behave better when its programs are on. Noise is reduced, and students are more likely to remain in their seats and more willing to follow school rules, according to the Web site. "Drivers used BusRadio as a behavioral tool. . . . If kids misbehaved, they lost the privilege of listening to the show," the Web site said.

BusRadio said that in test runs, its commercials were effective in attracting kids' attention. The WB network, for example, wanted to promote its television shows to kids. Print ads could reach the right audience but perhaps not on the day that the shows were to be broadcast. Commercial radio could do that, but it was considered inefficient for the youngest of viewers because kids "tend to turn the station when the ads begin."

WB tried BusRadio, running the promotions on the days the shows were scheduled to air and broadcasting more ads during the students' ride home "so they could reinforce the message to watch that night."

"It's a pretty clever concept," particularly because the company is using the issue of child safety to promote the concept, said Paul Kurnit, head of KidShop, a New York marketing firm that advises food companies on promoting products to children, [and former president of Griffin Bacal, an ad agency specializing in the children's market].

Kurnit, who learned of BusRadio just last week, said, "They are using traditional media to reach kids in an environment that up to now has been pretty noncommercial." And that, Kurnit said, could make the concept controversial, especially at a time when a growing number of health professionals and government officials are calling for restrictions on marketing products—particularly junk food—to children.

Kids, Ads, and Legislative Restrictions

Last month, the Department of Health and Human Services and the Federal Trade Commission called on the food industry to voluntarily set minimum nutrition standards for foods that can be marketed to children. Last year, the prestigious Institute of Medicine, part of the National Academies, said Con-

"Game-Vertising"

In-game advertising, or "game-vertising," is a highly sophisticated, finely tuned strategy that combines product placement, behavioral targeting and viral marketing to forge ongoing relationships between brands and individual gamers. Marketing through interactive games works particularly well for snack, beverage and other "impulse" food products. Coca-Cola, Pepsi, Mountain Dew, Gatorade, McDonald's, Burger King and KFC, for example, were the "most recalled brands" by video game players, according to an October 2006 survey conducted by Phoenix Marketing International. . . .

At a September 2006 conference on interactive advertising, software developers explained how they purposefully create games to make them "in sync with the brand," ensuring that images players see in the game are similar to what "they see in the supermarket aisle . . . [and on TV] Saturday morning."

At Viacom's Neopets.com—targeted at 8- to 17-year-olds—young gamers create and "take care of" virtual pets, earning virtual currency (neopoints) to pay for the pet's upkeep by participating in contests and games. The site earns substantial advertising revenues from "User Initiated Brand Integrated Advertising"—activities or games built around advertisers' products and services that help build relationships and generate revenues with Neopets visitors. For example, participants can earn points by buying or selling "valuable commodities," such as McDonald's french fries, or winning games with names like "Cinnamon Toast Crunch: The Umpire Strikes Out!"

Jeff Chester and Kathryn Montgomery,
"No Escape: Marketing to Kids in the Digital Age,"
Multinational Monitor, *July-August 2008.*

gress should mandate changes if food and beverage manufacturers fail to promote healthful products in the next two years. In 2004, in another report, the Institute of Medicine said schools should strive to be "as advertising-free as possible."

That could be challenging for many schools, which increasingly have relied on corporate sponsorships and free products—usually branded—to ease tight budgets. At the same time, marketers have been courting schools, eager to distinguish their products among the hundreds of others promoted to kids every week on TV, radio, the Internet and anywhere they congregate. Some school districts have accepted ads on the outside of school buses, but up to now, the inside has been sacrosanct.

That's why critics are lining up even before BusRadio is officially launched. "It's using the compulsory education law to compel kids to listen to ads," said Gary Ruskin, executive director of the public advocacy group Commercial Alert. "Its justification is it makes kids quiet. So what? They'd be quiet if we gave them cigarettes, but that doesn't mean we should."

Ruskin said he is also concerned about personal data the company will collect, particularly as kids go online to respond to contests and promotions. "Who gets the children's personal information?" he asked.

BusRadio Could Improve Bus Rides

Daniel Broughton, a pediatrician at the Mayo Clinic, said he was concerned that advertising "in this situation takes on the air of being official." That was one of the concerns many parents and advertising critics had when schools accepted free television and satellite dishes in exchange for free programming, including ads, from Channel One.

There are some differences from Channel One, Broughton noted, because BusRadio isn't aired during school, when it would divert teacher time or conflict with in-class programming.

BusRadio says on its Web site that its service is an improvement over what students hear if a bus driver listens to AM or FM radio. "It is virtually impossible to listen to commercial radio for 30 minutes without being offended by a song's lyrics or DJ's talk. . . . BusRadio entertains the students while virtually eliminating the concerns of inappropriate music, DJ talk and commercials."

Linda Farbry, director of transportation for Fairfax County public schools, said its buses are equipped with AM/FM radios precisely for students. "If they listen to music, they are controlled and quiet. . . . Some of these trips are long, and we want kids to do something other than pick on other kids."

The county has 22 stations it considers acceptable for student ears, such as soft rock WASH (97.1 FM) and country WMZQ (98.7 FM). Would Farbry consider BusRadio for her buses, which transport 110,000 students a day? "It depends on the cost," she said.

[Editor's note: BusRadio ceased operation in 2009.]

Periodical Bibliography

The following articles have been selected to supplement the diverse views presented in this chapter.

Robert Abelman
"Fighting the War on Indecency: Mediating TV, Internet, and Videogame Usage Among Achieving and Underachieving Gifted Children," *Roeper Review*, Winter 2007.

Nazli Baydar et al.
"Effects of an Educational Television Program on Preschoolers: Variability in Benefits," *Journal of Applied Developmental Psychology*, vol. 29, no. 5, September-October 2008.

Brooks Boliek
"FTC: Violence Still Marketed to Youths," *Hollywood Reporter*, April 13, 2007.

Andrew Gumbel
"The Hollywood Sting: Life in the Star Factory," *Independent* (United Kingdom), August 1, 2007.

D. Paul Harris
"Christian Video Games Remain Scarce, But Interest Growing," *St. Louis Post-Dispatch*, January 11, 2006.

Matthew L. Myers
"Alicia Keys Sets Example for Entertainment Industry by Withdrawing Tobacco Industry Sponsorship of Indonesia Concert," Campaign for Tobacco-Free Kids, July 28, 2008. www.tobaccofreekids.org.

Shaheen Pasha
"Children's Music Rocks," CNNMoney.com, March 1, 2006.

Diego Vasquez
"The Lowdown on How Teens Use Media," *Media Life*, June 30, 2009. www.medialifemagazine.com.

Mark Wheeler
"Study Uses Music to Explore the Autistic Brain's Emotion Processing," UCLA Newsroom, May 7, 2008.

OPPOSING
VIEWPOINTS®
SERIES

Are Children in the Entertainment Industry Exploited?

Chapter Preface

Twice in recent years, controversy has erupted in Australia regarding the age of runway fashion models. In 2007, fifteen-year-old Claire Quirk was pulled from the position as "the face" of the Melbourne Spring Fashion Week because of her age; that same year, twelve-year-old Maddison Gabriel was featured as the face of the Gold Coast Fashion Week. Some critics and parents objected to models so young by claiming that it sexually exploits children. Other critics—especially business people—argued that models too young would alienate the very shoppers the fashion shows hoped to attract: professional women in their thirties.

Child models are not new, of course. Children's clothing has been sold in catalogs as long as adult clothes have, and children have been posed wearing it in print and on television. Twelve-year-old girls and boys appear in ads for GapKids and other children's clothing stores on a daily basis without comment from child advocacy groups or the media. The fact that children model is almost entirely noncontroversial—in the world of children's fashion. In the world of adult fashion, however, designers and producers have been accused of sexually exploiting the girls who wear their clothes.

It is a gray area. Although many adults do seek out pictures of models just to look at attractive people (and thus may end up ogling models who are young teenagers), fashion models are paid to show off clothes. Their faces and bodies are not meant to be the primary focus of attention. Of course, bathing suit and underwear models stretch that boundary and blur the distinction, emphasizing the bodies as much as the outfits. Compare that to another industry that judges women by the clothes they wear: beauty pageants. In a beauty pageant's bathing suit or evening gown category, the contestant is judged specifically on how beautiful she looks in that clothing. Winners are regaled as objects of desire and admiration, and featured for months in public and print appearances that further draw attention to their sexual attractiveness. Winners of the Miss America pageant have been eighteen or older since at least 1980, but there are pageants for teenagers and children, too; the America's National Teenager pageant has a pre-teen division for girls as young as nine, and the World's Precious Children national pageant has divisions for babies younger than two. The reality television show *Toddlers & Tiaras* follows such infant competitors and their families through various events, and provides many examples of how even extremely young children are taught to imitate adult appearances and behaviors to impress adult judges.

Children have been appearing in movies and on television since the media were invented, and photographed and painted before that. It is not generally considered exploitative to hire a child actor to play a child character, or to use the image of a child to sell children's products. But some critics say child beauty pageants—and commercial television programs about them—turn children into the actual product for audience consumption. These critics claim these children are transformed by adults into objects that appeal to adults. They are marketed to adult audiences for profit, and they generally do not have the intellectual development or political ability to defend themselves.

The following chapter explores the different ways that adults establish children in entertainment industry careers, how they define and nurture child performers' talents and skills, and how children's lives benefit or suffer from adult intervention.

"'I've only had two kids who got into trouble. All the rest were clean and went to college.'"

Talent Agents Have Child Performers' Best Interests at Heart

David Mermelstein

David Mermelstein writes on a range of entertainment industry topics, for a variety of publications, from Variety *to the* Wall Street Journal. *The following viewpoint first appeared in the 2008* Youth Impact Report *of* Variety *magazine, a supplement that highlights the year's young stars and the Hollywood professionals—from casting directors and music producers to lawyers—who support them. This profile is of Judy Savage, head of the Savage Agency, a talent agent who transitioned from the role of "stage mother" to actors' representative, after raising three children of her own who were actors.*

David Mermelstein, "Decades of Nurturing Know-How: How Parenthood Taught Judy Savage to Groom Showbiz Kids," *Daily Variety,* vol. 300, October 3, 2008, p. A51. Reproduced by permission.

As you read, consider the following questions:

1. According to the author, why does Judy Savage say that it was her oldest son who got her into her career as a talent agent?

2. As cited by Mermelstein, why won't Savage sign children whose parents want them to act more than they do?

3. What changes in the entertainment industry does Savage blame for the current cutthroat climate among actors' representatives, according to the viewpoint?

Judy Savage has been representing child actors for 30 years, heading up the Savage Agency, the longest-running youth-focused talent agency to withstand being gobbled up by one of the major firms. But if you turned the clock back and asked a younger Judy what she wanted to be when she grew up, you'd get a very different answer.

Like a real-life Juno MacGuff [teenage character in the movie *Juno*], Savage faced an unanticipated pregnancy at age 16. She finished high school by correspondence, and then earned a college degree in biology while raising three kids. In a sense, it was her eldest son, Mark, who chose Savage's current career for her with his desire to perform onstage at a young age.

A natural entertainer, Mark landed a part in the road company of *Mame*, starring Celeste Holm in the role originated by Angela Lansbury. When the young actor was called to Los Angeles to appear in the show opposite Lansbury herself, the move prompted Savage to recast her family's destiny and focus on showbiz.

"I realized we were all having so much fun," Savage recalls from behind a large desk in her cozy Hollywood office. "So we sold our house in Detroit and moved to L.A. We had no jobs, but I had written ahead to agents, and after the first day, we had one. Three days later, the kids had jobs." What followed, besides divorce from the father of her children, was a whirli-gig life of casting calls, rehearsals and shoots, with all three of Savage's children—not just Mark, but also Tracie and Brad—variously involved in stage shows, commercials and movies.

From Managing Family to Managing Clients

Mark, who today writes musicals and runs IT [information technology] at the Savage Agency, continued performing through his teens, taking his final bow in a Florida production of *Hello, Dolly*. Brad, currently a marketing veep at NBC Universal, appeared in nine movies and 167 commercials by the time he was 11, pulling the plug on his acting career after 1984's *Red Dawn*. Tracie made numerous guest appearances on TV series before becoming a news reporter, now at KFWB radio, but she still enjoys the occasional TV cameo.

"Tracie's competition was fierce," Savage says. "This is a much harder business for young girls because there are so many more of them trying out. There are twice as many things for boys and only half as many of them."

Although Savage built her agency on the experience that came from being mother to three child actors, she initially met resistance from the very pros she already knew, rather than finding open doors. "Trying to get these casting directors who knew me as a mother, not as an agent, to see me as a professional wasn't easy," she recalls.

She persevered, though, buying a small bungalow on a side street in Hollywood for $40,000 and then setting up shop there in early 1978—it remains the Savage Agency's home to this day. "The first four or five years were horrible," she ac-knowledges. "But each year, I'd do a little bit better." Early on, she made ends meet by flipping houses in the then-flush real estate market. She was also lucky enough to be solidly posi-tioned for what she calls "the best years for children" in net-work TV—the 1980s and the '90s. "Think about all those ABC shows that featured kids, and those shows lasted for eight years each," says Savage, who always puts kids' interests first when signing new clients—which is more than can be said for many stage moms.

"I interview the parents and the kids very closely to make sure (acting) is a passion for the kids," she says. "If the parents want it and the kids don't, we don't want them. If baseball's your passion, play baseball. They need the passion and the look."

Her protective, mother-hen quality comes across immediately in person—a plaque in her photograph-filled office proclaims, "Nothing you do for children is ever wasted," and she backs up such sentiments by noting of her clients, "I've only had two kids who got into trouble. All the rest were clean and went to college."

Doing Business in a Niche Market

Her biggest foe seems to be the aging process—not just because her clients grow up and leave the business when they reach young adulthood, but also because those who continue acting tend to defect to larger agencies with more diverse portfolios.

"These big agents shower these kids with gifts and promises," she says. "Lucas Grabeel (of *High School Musical* fame) is the exception."

Yet even in her own niche, business can be cutthroat. "When I started, people didn't poach," she says. "We were all friends. We even informed each other when we were approached by one another's clients. It's much more competitive now."

She attributes these changes largely to economic woes. "Because of the strikes, almost half our commercial business went away. And because California doesn't give tax credits, we're losing shows every year," she explains.

New York State Laws Protect Young Entertainers

The statute in New York specifically mandates that the court inquire as to the overall contract being "in the best interest of the child." For this reason, an employer should be aware that, often, in addition to salary and related expenses such as hotel and travel, the employer is usually responsible for the cost of tutoring and other educational needs of the minor, particularly if the services required under the contract will prevent the minor from attending his or her regular school. Generally, it is recommended to an employer who will require a minor to tour, record in a studio or be present on a movie set that he ascertain the nature of the educational or tutoring requirements and the costs to pay for them, at the time that the contract is initially negotiated.

New York courts will also consider the nature of the work and type of services to be performed when reviewing a contract for approval. Often the content involved (sexual content, violence or dangerous stunts), the time frame and the age of the minor will all weigh heavily on deciding whether a contract meets the "best interests of the minor."

Diane Krausz,
"Protecting Young Talent in the Entertainment Business,"
New York Law Journal, *April 14, 2005.*

Yet the news is far from all bad. Lately, Savage has been involved in what appears to be a mutually beneficial relationship with Paradigm, the large, Beverly Hills-based talent agency. "Paradigm didn't want the hassles of a children's department, so they came to us," she says.

"When I think somebody's about to jump ship, they take a look, and if they take them on, we split the fees 50-50. Right now, we're sharing Zach Mills."

After 30 years of looking after others, Savage is finally thinking about looking after herself a bit more. She's taken on a partner, Stella Alex, to whom she's ultimately selling the Savage Agency. "I'll always be here if they need me," Savage says. But she also is making time for things that her 30-year, full-time job didn't always permit: gardening, seeing more of her grandchildren and teaching weekend seminars on the subject she knows best.

"I'm even thinking of starting a clothing line for older folks," she adds. "You know, the population is aging."

> *"Debbie McGee has been touring the country signing up young hopefuls, some of whom got precisely nothing—other than a few snapshots—in return for their money."*

Talent Agents Sometimes Deceive Hopeful Child Performers

Zoe Brennan

Zoe Brennan is a feature writer for the Daily Mail, *the first newspaper in the United Kingdom (UK) to sell a million copies a day; she was previously the Westminster correspondent at the* Sunday Times, *another UK publication. The following viewpoint describes the possibly shady, at best incompetent, talent agent Debbie McGee, founder of a now defunct, "rogue" talent agency that collected money from child-model hopefuls and delivered almost no work to any of them. McGee defends herself by saying that one cannot guarantee modeling work; critics claim legitimate agencies do not charge fees in advance, especially for photographs.*

As you read, consider the following questions:

1. According to Brennan, why did parents and children believe that Debbie McGee would be a good agent for a modeling or acting hopeful?

2. What evidence suggests that Debbie McGee is more interested in making money than working as a children's talent agent, as described by the author?

3. As cited by Brennan, what evidence suggests that McGee's business was not ever going to help modeling and acting hopefuls find industry work?

This is a magic trick with a difference. Starstruck, the blonde, blue-eyed little girl moved forward to speak to her idols.

Her proud mother looked on as television magician Paul Daniels and his wife, the lovely Debbie McGee, signed pictures of themselves for the delighted ten-year-old and assured her she had a glittering career as a model before her.

Then, while little Gina Barlow was prepared for a photo session for her portfolio at the Roundhouse Hotel in Bournemouth, her mother, Andrea, was taken aside to pay £125—a small fee given on the understanding that it might open the doors to a glittering showbiz career, either in TV or modelling.

McGee told Mrs Barlow: "I've got a massive address book full of casting agents and directors that Paul and I have accumulated over the years."

Paul nodded proudly, and McGee's own mother stood by to meet Gina and other similarly excited youngsters, leading the assembled would-be stars to believe they were in safe hands.

McGee said: "If anyone can get your daughter work, I can."

A Scam or a Fickle Business?

It was not to be, however. Gina did not receive any work and her mother believes they were victims of a cruel scam.

"I trusted Paul and Debbie," she says. "They are so famous. I thought they had to be genuine when I saw Debbie advertising for young models in the paper.

"When I realised we'd given them £125, I felt stupid."

Worse still was watching her daughter's dreams turn to ashes.

Andrea says: "She had even spent some of her own pocket money on the fee.

"Children feel these things ten times more than adults. You build yourself up and it doesn't work out—she's just given up now.

"She's become quite withdrawn. Debbie and Paul made a quick buck out of my daughter's dreams."

But how can this be? Surely Debbie McGee and Paul Daniels are treasured household names, British entertainers from the golden days of variety shows?

Sadly, it appears that the couple are not quite as straightforward as they seem, for the Barlows are not alone in their experience.

Debbie McGee has been touring the country signing up young hopefuls, some of whom got precisely nothing—other than a few snapshots—in return for their money.

Another mother, who did not wish to be named, says: "We too got stung.

"My daughter went to one of these sessions at York—we paid £150.

"Debbie McGee was there to greet us and seemed nice. Then, when we had questions to ask after we paid, she had no time, because her mum and dad turned up.

"We heard nothing until a month ago, then received a letter saying she was no longer running the company and someone else had taken over.

"To stay involved you had to pay another joining fee—surprise, surprise."

Debbie McGee Models stopped trading at Christmas [2007], leaving those who had signed up in the lurch.

For her part, McGee, 49, says: "Unfortunately, mothers think their daughters are going to be stars, but it's not that easy. The business is fickle."

McGee's Own Career in Entertainment

Business was not so fickle for McGee, however. She signed up 400 youngsters over a year—turning over £50,000 in "photographer's fees" alone.

She herself did very well out of the "fickle" business, becoming a household name as Paul's glamorous magic assistant.

Clad in her sequined costumes, life under the stage lights was a world away from her childhood.

Born in Kingston upon Thames, Surrey, in 1958, her parents ran a corner shop.

The ambitious Debbie won a place at the Royal Ballet School.

She "was actually offered places with a couple of big European ballet companies, but I decided to accept at the Iranian National Ballet. I was mercenary because they were paying the most money—double what the Royal Ballet corps de ballet were."

So off she went to Iran, performing *Swan Lake* for the shah while beady-eyed guards with machine guns stood in the wings.

After this, she auditioned to appear in the *Paul Daniels Magic Show*, where she met her future husband.

Their marriage has endured accusations of her gold digging—most famously with comedienne Mrs Merton's question: "So, what first attracted you to the millionaire Paul Daniels?" . . .

However, recently there have been reports the couple have been hit by financial trouble.

Certainly, McGee seemed eager to make money from her agency.

She and Paul swopped their Buckinghamshire mansion, once owned by Roger Moore, for a smaller home on the banks of the Thames, called Toad Hall.

The Ferrari they drove in the eighties, with the number-plate MAG1C, is long gone.

His glory days as the king of light entertainment are over and they have been doing the rounds of D-list celebrity shows—from *Celebrity Wife Swap* to *Battle of the Stars*.

The couple are even resorting to selling possessions on Internet auction site eBay.

Recently, McGee posted a size eight dress from High Street chain Karen Millen, describing it as "a real eye-catcher" and advertising it as: "Worn by Debbie McGee on the final night of *Celebrity X Factor* 2006 and only worn once since then."

It sold for £81, with a second dress achieving the grand price of £25.

Her most recent sale was an "'elegant Moschino black two-piece suit", asking for starting bids of £50.

She says she sells on eBay "because it's great, it's fun".

But could the cash also be a factor? The question to Debbie elicits an immediate telephone call from Daniels, who says they do it "not really" for money, but "to make space in the house".

Asked if he is under financial pressure, he says: "You're kidding."

Financial Motivations Complicate the Picture

Now, of course, he may well be right given his glittering career in the eighties and nineties, but it is fair to say the pair have a chequered financial past.

They lost a fortune ten years ago on McGee's touring ballet company Ballet Imaginaire, which cost them well over £150,000.

Another of the couple's companies, Magic Marketing Ltd—which was a venture to sell Paul's 'educational' course—promised to teach the tricks of his trade.

It was set up in the late eighties, but it filed its last accounts in 1997 and was dissolved in late 2000.

Its last accounts make sombre reading—amount owed to creditors, £124,000; total assets, £40,000; net liabilities, £84,000.

Daniels also has a 4 per cent stake in a computer company called Frooition Ltd, based in Stourbridge. It showed just £20,637 net assets in 2005–06.

But what of his wife's money-making efforts—in particular Debbie McGee Models?

The most recently filed reports for the company—set up under Debbie's married name, Debra Ann Daniels—show it has hardly been a success.

Set up with her business partner Sue Simons in June 2006, it is 51 per cent owned by McGee.

It returned net assets of just £608 in 2006/2007, and no salaries were paid to directors.

Companies House records show the business is still registered.

Wealth watchdog and *Sunday Times* Rich List compiler Dr Philip Beresford says: "There is no real money in this company. It was a case of trading off a celebrity name—but the Daniels name is so devalued there is nothing to trade off. It's a bit tacky."

The company is registered to an accountant's office in Bristol.

Its Web site has shut down and clients have been sent a letter telling them their details have been sent to another agency.

However, McGee's letter declined to name that agency.

Talent Agencies: Just the Facts

Q: What is the difference between a legitimate talent agency and one whose purpose is to separate you from your money?

A: The legitimate talent agency does not charge a fee payable in advance for registration, for resumes, public relations services, screen tests, photographs or acting lessons. If you are signed as a client by a reputable talent agency, you will pay nothing until you work. A commission of 10 to 15 percent of your earnings must be agreed upon in advance.

Most legitimate talent agencies do not advertise for clients in newspapers nor do they solicit through the mail, the Internet or by approaching you at shopping malls.

Q: Are reportable talent agencies licensed by the state of California?

A: Yes. Such talent agencies are licensed by the state as artists' managers and most established agencies in the motion picture and television industries are also franchised by the Screen Actors Guild. You should be extremely careful of any talent agency not licensed in your state.

Q: What about personal managers and business managers?

A: There are well-established firms in the business of personal management and business management. Such firms, however, typically handle established artists and do not advertise for new clients.

Jo Kelly, The Truth About Being an Extra.
Huntington Beach, CA: August II Productions, 2006.

An Agency Doomed to Fail

One person with an intriguing insight into the workings of the agency is the broadcaster Vanessa Feltz, who appeared on *Celebrity Wife Swap* with McGee and Daniels in 2007.

She says: "Debbie represented herself as some sort of business mogul, but during the entire week we devoted just 20 minutes to her agency.

"I saw no staff and it looked like a miserable Web site with a few extremely ordinary people on it."

She adds: "I wasn't aware of a single phone call coming in to the agency while I was there.

"I can't say whether it was a scam or not, but it wasn't a hive of activity."

Perhaps it is no wonder McGee has bailed out. She denies that the agency was a scam, saying: "I haven't had anything to do with the agency since the end of November.

"I'm a hands-on person and I've got too busy."

Regarding charging young hopefuls up-front fees, she says: "The £125 was not to join the agency, that was for the photographs and being on my Web site for a year.

"If they had brought their own professional photos, I would have used those instead.

"There were a handful of people who, for whatever reason, didn't get any work.

"I feel sad that Andrea Barlow and her daughter were disappointed, but I think she hadn't understood that her fee wasn't for joining the agency, it was for the photographs.

"We really worked hard for every person."

She would not say how many people received genuine work through Debbie McGee Models, but claims she sought guidance from the actors' union Equity on her fees.

Just Another "Rogue" Agency

Clive Hurst, an actor who campaigns against rogue talent agencies, says: "Debbie McGee is talking rubbish.

"It does not cost £125 to take rough snapshots of youngsters.

"Legitimate model agencies do not take up-front fees. They only work with people who are genuinely talented, and charge when they have found the individuals work.

"This is totally unethical. These people were taken in by Debbie McGee and these unfortunate children were easy money for her."

Just like Daniels's magic tricks, it is hard to get to the bottom of Debbie McGee Models through talking to the magical maestro.

He telephones to set the record straight for his wife, saying first: "I have to say, I am out of this, I was just there as a consultant.

"We've had just one complaint and that was a doting showbiz mother really.

"I've got a beautiful granddaughter—I'm sure she's going to be a star. We are all guilty of that with our kids."

Asked whether he thinks it is right to trade on those proud parents and grandparents, taking £125 from each family, he says: "Whoa, whoa, whoa now!

"We had people coming to us who had already paid over £250 for other photo sessions—they would not be able to get a photo session at the price Debbie was charging.

"We never made a penny from these interviews. We hoped to make money on getting them bookings, but in showbiz, getting bookings is really difficult."

The fact remains that Daniels and McGee took up-front payment for children who did not then see their dreams come true.

For now, however, this magical vanishing act would appear to be over.

> *"If an actor wants to be a recording artist, an author or star in a TV movie, or even produce, . . . these opportunities are made available to them."*

Production Studios Foster the Careers of Child Stars

Rebecca Ascher-Walsh

Rebecca Ascher-Walsh is a journalist who has written for many different newspapers, magazines, blogs, and trade publications, including Hollywood Reporter. *The following viewpoint explores how many of the children's entertainment networks, such as Disney Channel and Nickelodeon, fully invest in the child actors that they believe can be stars. Ascher-Walsh contends that these young entertainers learn the business and grow as performers in safe environments that nurture their talents and expand their interests—opportunities not afforded to most adults working in music, film, or television.*

As you read, consider the following questions:

1. According to the author, how are child entertainers of today treated differently by the studios than they were twenty years ago?

2. How does promoting child actors across mediums (such as putting television stars into movies) benefit the studios who employ them, as noted by the author?

3. As described by the author, how does working within a studio increase a child actor's chances of continuing to work when he or she becomes an adult?

Youth has always been a marketable virtue in Hollywood, but never more so than today. That doesn't mean the most-valued stars are fretting over their next Botox injections, though. Indeed, many of them are still waiting for puberty to hit.

While film studios grapple with keeping budgets down, and TV networks try to plot their winning prime-time line-ups, outlets devoted to children's and tween programming are raking in enormous bucks and winning the kind of fan base that even adult A-listers rarely enjoy. The general public eventually hears of these young talents once they "break out" into the adult world—think of Hilary Duff, Lindsay Lohan and Mary-Kate and Ashley Olsen—but for millions of kids, those names are so five minutes ago.

Who matters now? Raven [Raven-Symoné]. Miley Cyrus. Emma Roberts. Lil' JJ. These are only some of the stars being created by the behemoth Disney Channel and Nickelodeon [Nick] and, to some extent, by studios such as Walden Media and New Line Cinema and channels such as Discovery Kids and MTV's new offshoot the N [currently known as Teen Nick]. But regardless of the talent or the show, what unites all of these companies is a modern strategy built on the understanding that these days, a one-off deal is child's play.

"I think that Disney got smart after the *Mickey Mouse Club* with Britney Spears and Christina Aguilera, where they didn't have them under contract," says agent Cindy Osbrink of the Osbrink Agency, which has clients on shows for Discovery Kids, the N and Nickelodeon. "Now, Disney and Nickelodeon include several components in their deals. They want the whole package."

And that seems to be suiting the kids just fine. Says producer Tom Lynch, who created Nickelodeon's *The Secret World of Alex Mack*, one of the first series to be aimed at the tween market, as well as current series *South of Nowhere* for the N and *Romeo!* for Nickelodeon: "Twenty years ago, you had the *Mickey Mouse Club*, or you had what I call the 'Crest kids with big smiles,'" he says. "At that point, the idea of launching a 'career' wasn't in the psyche. It was about just finding a place to work, and kids were relegated to really bad animation or wraparounds. Then, Nickelodeon came into play, and Disney blew up.

"Today," Lynch continues, "you're seeing kids with a game plan. It begins with Nickelodeon and Disney and then goes into touring with a band and then on to movies."

What makes the transition relatively seamless are audiences that will follow their idols from medium to medium. "If you end up on a Disney Channel or a Nickelodeon series, that will be your fan base, and they'll grow up alongside you," explains Matt Fletcher, head of the youth division at Acme Talent & Literary Agency, who also represents Chelsea Harris of Nickelodeon's upcoming *Just Jordan* and Malese Jow of Nick's *Unfabulous*. "Landing a client at those networks is about career longevity.

"They're really good about finding the kid who stands out and taking advantage of it in a good way," he adds.

Even from the beginning of a show's development, young talent who find a niche at these channels can enjoy an advantage unknown to even the most bankable adult sitcom star.

"We focus," Disney Channel president of entertainment Gary Marsh says simply. While a broadcast network might have hundreds of shows in development, Nickelodeon and Disney hone in on only a dozen or so. And once they hit the air, it's not uncommon for Disney and Nickelodeon to commit for years (in contrast with the networks, which might commit to a mere handful of episodes). "The great thing about Nick and Disney is that if a pilot gets picked up there, as opposed to a network, it's usually for three years, so you don't have to worry that every seven episodes you're about to get canceled," Osbrink says.

The greenlighting of a show, thanks to all-inclusive deals, is just the beginning of opportunities for the starring talent. "With Nickelodeon and Disney, the key words are synergy," says Mitchell Gossett, director of the youth division at Cunningham-Escott-Slevin-Doherty [CESD] and the agent of Cyrus, the eponymous star of Disney Channel's *Hannah Montana*. "These are corporate giants with film divisions, music and TV, and the smart agents know how to manipulate that synergy correctly."

In the case of Disney, Marsh says, "What's happened in the last five years is that the channel has become a talent incubator for the whole company to build new franchises. If an actor wants to be a recording artist, an author or star in a TV movie, or even produce as was the case with Raven, these opportunities are made available to them."

It's a win-win for both the talent and the companies.

"If I can take a person like Miley Cyrus and create a touring act that will potentially create a feature-film role, then that's goodwill to the channel," Marsh says. "The talent gains financially, but there's also tremendous exposure not only for the talent but for the show." In addition to a record deal, Cyrus landed a vocal role in Disney Channel's animated series *The Replacements*, while Ashley Tisdale (*The Suite Life of Zack & Cody*) scored a role in the phenomenally successful Disney

A College That Grooms Student Musicians for Success

The Academy of Contemporary Music [ACM], recent recipient of a Queen's Award for Innovation in Education, is redefining the way music is taught in [the United Kingdom]. It has, over the years, established such strong links with the industry it always hoped to serve that the two are now practically indivisible: New students enter, aged 18, through the door marked "College," and exit, two years later, through the revolving door and straight into the music biz. . . .

We should not, perhaps, be so surprised to learn in the 21st century that rock stardom is now something you can effectively learn. We are, after all, living in an age of reality television-produced pop stars, where we get to see the young, the gauche and the inexperienced often groomed for just that. But while so many of these programmes' contestants subsequently flail in the spotlight, often crushed by the weight of their own naïveté, graduates of ACM hope to arrive into the industry much more sussed [prepared].

"Our main aim here," confirms Mark Bound, the college's A&R [artist and repertoire] consultant, "is not simply to teach them about the industry but also to be aware of all the possible pitfalls. We want to demystify its appeal to some extent, in the hope that they will be ready for whatever comes, both good and bad."

Nick Duerden,
"Who Needs Simon Cowell? Enrol at the School
Where Fame and Fortune Are Part of the Curriculum,"
Independent *(United Kingdom), May 3, 2009.*

Channel original movie *High School Musical* and a voice-over role in the upcoming animated series *Phineas and Ferb*. Raven, who has had an association with Disney for the past seven years, has parlayed her success in the hit series *That's So Raven* into roles in the 2003 telefilm *The Cheetah Girls*, the 2004 family comedy *The Princess Diaries 2: Royal Engagement* and this year's *The Cheetah Girls 2*. In addition, she has recorded two albums for Disney Records and *This Is My Time* for Hollywood Records.

Nickelodeon follows a similar model, taking advantage of its relationships with other divisions at Viacom. "There's an active synergy within the company," says Paula Kaplan, who oversees the channel's casting division. "I talk to the head of casting at Paramount on a regular basis, and we have a record deal with Sony BMG." Those close relationships helped Josh Peck of Nick's *Drake & Josh* land a role in Owen Wilson's upcoming comedy *Drillbit Taylor*, for Paramount, and scored [Emma] Roberts, the star of the net's *Unfabulous*, a record deal at Sony; Nick Cannon, whose career was launched with Nick's *All That* back in 1998, went on to serve as a writer on the net's *Kenan & Kel* and as the creator of *The Nick Cannon Show*; he's now developing a show for MTV.

Recently, voice-over work also has gained importance in a star's overall deal as Disney and Nickelodeon ramp up their animated series and features. "People talk about looking for triple threats—kids who are actors, singers and dancers," Disney Channel senior veep of original programming Adam Bonnett says. "We're looking for quadruple threats, which means kids who can also be voice-over talent." CESD's voice-over division has nine full-time agents devoted solely to placing clients in sound studios.

Executives insist that all-encompassing deals don't equal velvet handcuffs. "It's not like we own you," says Marsh, "but the model is very self-evident, dating back to Hilary Duff. We create deals like no one else. We say to our talent, 'You have the next 30 years to grow older, so take advantage of what you have now.'" To hear Cyrus tell it, the atmosphere is indeed nurturing rather than claustrophobic. "For me, singing is always my No. 1 passion, so I'm happy to be in a studio and have the freedom to pursue that, but also in a safe environment," she says. "At Disney, the audience gets to know you, and not just your character. It's very comforting to know the company will take care of me as long as I do good things. I'm just a beginner, and they're really guiding me."

Also eager to keep talent in-house are companies such as Walden and New Line, which, like Disney and Nickelodeon, take advantage of corporate tie-ins when it comes to promoting their young actors. Walden has a production deal with FOX, as well as a book deal with Penguin Group, while New Line is part of the Time Warner family. "When you put a client in any production, whether it's at Disney or Paramount or Nickelodeon or NBC, they're always going to look at their source of talent that's worked in the past and pool from that," Fletcher explains. "This is a business, and we all want to make money, so the studios will hire those who give solid performances."

Which isn't to say a star who lands outside of the Disney or Nickelodeon systems would be lost. Take, for example, Cassie Scerbo and Carolina Carattini, two members of Slumber Party Girls, a five-girl band that hosts CBS's Saturday morning kids' programming block. "They're also a music group," says Margot Klar, their agent at CESD, "so they have a record deal with Geffen and are looking for their own series."

An entree into a studio also can mean a chance for child actors to work outside of all-kid casts on a more consistent basis. As Mark Kaufman, New Line's executive veep of production and theater, explains, "Look at Dakota Fanning. We found her and created her with (2001's) *I Am Sam*. And we're actively looking for projects to do with her again." New Line's *Take the Lead* star Elijah Kelley has been cast in the studio's upcoming production of *Hairspray*, and Kaufman is already looking for another New Line project for *Hairspray* star Zac Efron. (The movie also will have a tie-in soundtrack.) "We always want to get a second movie out of our talent, and we're always on the lookout for new talent," Kaufman says. "As cliche as it sounds, we consider ourselves a family, and if you've done a movie here, we'll want to do another."

But for all the synergy now available, talent who has yet to gain a foothold in a media conglomerate has no reason to lose heart—even if they can't sing and dance. "I think you can totally just be an actor," Fletcher says. "A lot of times, actors who want to do everything—it takes a toll on them. It's like when you're a kid playing sports. If you try to play every one, you won't be the best at any of them." And then, of course, there's the old-fashioned element of entertainment that no amount of strategizing can beat. "Sometimes," says Lynch, "the best thing you can do for talent is just to leave the door open. And then all you have to do is wait and see what magic happens."

| "[Miley] Cyrus is part of a long line of teen stars over the years who have struggled to balance their child-like appeal with their changing hormones."

Child Stars Are Held to Unreasonable Standards

Caitriona Palmer

Caitriona Palmer is a journalist for Independent.ie, Ireland's largest news source on the Internet. The following viewpoint describes the controversy that erupted after the fifteen-year-old performer, Miley Cyrus, posed with a bare back and then again with a bare midriff for Vanity Fair *magazine. Cyrus, popular with children and their parents for her clean image and wholesome appeal, was heavily criticized for being too sexual, but also held up as an innocent victim of exploitation by a fashion magazine.*

As you read, consider the following questions:

1. As described in the viewpoint, before Miley Cyrus posed for *Vanity Fair*, how was she perceived by the public?

2. How does the *Vanity Fair* photographer defend the pictures of Miley Cyrus, as explained by the author?

3. According to the author, what two contradictory demands for female behavior put adolescent stars like Miley Cyrus in such difficult public positions?

She is as sweet and as wholesome as American apple pie. But this week [in 2008] teen pop sensation Miley Cyrus discovered just how bitter the taste of celebrity life can sometimes be.

The 15-year-old star of the Disney Channel hit TV show *Hannah Montana* was forced to apologise after a provocative photograph of her hit the newsstands on Wednesday in the June edition of *Vanity Fair* magazine.

"I took part in a photo shoot that was supposed to be 'artistic' and now, seeing the photographs and reading the story, I feel so embarrassed," Cyrus said in a statement issued through her publicist. "I never intended for any of this to happen and I apologise to my fans who I care so deeply about."

The photograph in question, shot by celebrated photographer Annie Leibovitz, showed the church-going teenager apparently nude and wrapped in a satin bed sheet, her bare back exposed with a Lolita-esque 'come hither' look on her face.

Another photograph shows the young singer flashing a bare midriff while resting on the knee of her father, "Achy Breaky Heart" country singer Billy Ray Cyrus. Cyrus, who skyrocketed to fame playing an ordinary teenager who leads a double life as a rock star on *Hannah Montana*, is beloved by millions of pre-pubescent fans and their parents for her wholesome appeal and fresh-faced charm.

Nicknamed 'Miley' by her family for her 'smiley' demeanour, Cyrus made her Disney debut at 13 and became an instant overnight success. Her father's flagging career was revived when he was cast to play opposite her as Hannah Montana's on-screen dad.

The richest child entertainer in America, according to *People* magazine, Cyrus is projected to earn more than $1bn [billion] by the time she turns 18. Her first two albums debuted at number one on the charts and a film version of her concert tour grossed over $60 million in the box office—an unheard of feat for a concert movie.

Cyrus took home $20 million alone from her 2007 tour and recently signed a seven-figure deal to write a book about her short life.

Far more popular than Britney [Spears] ever was, her 70-date concert tour last year sold out in minutes, leaving normally well-connected people like Barack Obama scrambling for tickets.

The demand for tickets was so great that some parents resorted to whacky endurance contests—like hanging on a pole for six days.

But her photo spread has punctured her image as the innocent girl next door, alarming parents who believed she was different from the disgraced Britney.

Did *Vanity Fair* Exploit a Minor

"MILEY'S SHAME" screamed the *New York Post*, as *Vanity Fair* moved quickly to dispel the uproar saying that both Cyrus and her guardians had approved the nude Leibovitz shot. "Miley's parents and/or minders were on the set all day," said *Vanity Fair* spokeswoman Beth Kseniak. "Since the photo was taken digitally, they saw it on the shoot and everyone thought it was a beautiful and natural portrait of Miley."

"In fact, when [*Vanity Fair* writer] Bruce Handy interviewed Miley, he asked her about the photo and she was very cheerful about it and thought it was perfectly fine."

Cyrus's publicist denied that her parents ever saw any images of the photo, saying that they left the set at the end of the day before the controversial picture was taken.

"I think it's really artsy," Cyrus is quoted as saying in the magazine. "It wasn't in a skanky way. Annie took, like, a beautiful shot, and I thought that was really cool. That's what she

Harry Potter, Naked

Every night in a London theatre, Daniel Radcliffe shows an audience of 900 that he has well and truly grown up. And his bosses at Warner Bros. aren't going to like it a bit. The US company makes the Harry Potter films in which Radcliffe stars as the boy wizard who became a national treasure in the books of J.K. Rowling. Now he is appearing full-frontal as a boy who smokes, has sex and mutilates horses, and Warner Bros. is slightly worried about its brand image.

With the fifth movie in the series, *Harry Potter and the Order of the Phoenix*, due to be released in July [2009], bosses are worried that audiences will see rather more of young Harry than is strictly necessary. "I guess we always knew that Harry and Daniel would have to grow up," said one source, "but we hadn't bargained on full-frontal sex scenes."

Katy Guest,
"Who Owns Daniel Radcliffe? The Curse of Child Fame,"
Independent *(United Kingdom), March 4, 2007.*

wanted me to do, and you can't say no to Annie. She's so cute. She gets this puppy dog look and you're like, 'OK,'" she said.

Disney Channel executives did not see the photo as "artsy" and suggested that *Vanity Fair* and Leibovitz were out to exploit a hapless young girl.

"Unfortunately, as the article suggests, a situation was created to deliberately manipulate a 15-year-old in order to sell magazines," a network statement said.

Leibovitz, renown for her iconic photos of the rich and famous—including a nude, pregnant Demi Moore—defended her photograph.

"I'm sorry that my portrait of Miley has been misinterpreted," she said in a statement.

"Miley and I looked at fashion photographs together and we discussed the picture in that context before we shot it. The photograph is a simple, classic portrait, shot with very little makeup, and I think it is very beautiful."

A Storm of Public Criticism

The *Vanity Fair* photographs would not have hogged the headlines so much had it not been for some other attention-grabbing shots of Cyrus posted on the Internet last week.

These amateur photos showed the teenager tugging down her tank top to show a hint of a bright green bra and draped languidly over the lap of her then boyfriend with her stomach bared.

Parents who have spent inordinate time and money on Cyrus tickets and merchandise for their children had reassured themselves this pop star was a safe bet, with no sex or drugs in the message.

But now they feel betrayed by the teenager's sultry photos, slamming the star on her MySpace page. "Miley I am the mother of an almost seven-year-old," wrote a woman called Amy. "I am wondering what choices you will make next. Up until now I haven't questioned your integrity. My daughter loves you."

"I don't agree with the photos. Please if you are a Christian then carry yourself in a more modest way."

A 15-year-old fan wrote: "Those pictures were really slutty. You're losing a lot of fans doing that stuff. If you keep it up you're going to be like Britney Spears."

Adolescent Stars Are Adolescents First

But despite analogies to Spears—to whom the term 'train wreck' rather than 'superstar' is now more commonly applied—some commentators say that it is unrealistic to market a burgeoning young adult as a squeaky clean role model to seven- and eight-year-olds.

"I think that Disney and Miley Cyrus's camp are trying to whitewash [Miley's] image and when you do that there is only a matter of time before there is graffiti," Monica Corcoran, a style editor at the *Los Angeles Times* told the *Irish Independent*.

At 15, Cyrus is beginning to understand her sexuality, says feminist commentator Germaine Greer. "Sexually knowing 15-year-olds are normal," she wrote in the *Guardian* this week. "No matter how much energy Disney . . . might put into denying the obvious, 15-year-olds are sexually aware."

Others disagreed, saying Cyrus had been exploited and that her parents and minders should have known better. "She is a young girl. She shouldn't have to deal with any of this," said Hollywood actress Jamie Lee Curtis, a former child star.

"I don't feel that she was duped . . . there were people at the shoot that should have been looking out to make sure this didn't happen," Curtis wrote in the Huffington Post blog.

Cyrus is part of a long line of teen stars over the years who have struggled to balance their child-like appeal with their changing hormones amid the onslaught of a sexually charged pop culture.

Vanessa Hudgens—star of Disney's smash-hit *High School Musical*—fell from grace when nude photos of her showed up on the Internet.

And Spears's sister, actress Jamie Lynn Spears, saw her wholesome television image crumble after she became pregnant at the tender age of 16.

Child stars like Cyrus seem trapped between two unhealthy extremes, either pushed into overtly sexual roles at a vulnerable age or forced to live up to a fairy-tale myth with puberty censored out of the picture.

According to Corcoran, Disney's reaction to Cyrus's photos was an attempt to preserve "the next Snow White."

"You look at a lot of these child stars that come out on hard times like Britney Spears and I think Disney really like[s] to trap these kids in amber to try and preserve this image," said Corcoran.

"But I think that when these kids start to grow up it's just unreasonable. It doesn't make sense."

Periodical Bibliography

The following articles have been selected to supplement the diverse views presented in this chapter.

Decca Aitkenhead
: "You've Been Very, Very Naughty," *Guardian* (United Kingdom), July 22, 2006.

Samara Kalk Derby
: "Talent Scout on Lookout for Healthy Self-Image," *Capital Times* (Madison, WI), February 18, 2009.

Patrick Foster
: "New Laws Could Mean Children Disappear from TV, Say Broadcasters," *Times Online* (United Kingdom), August 15, 2009.

Ali Frick
: "Coal Industry Exploits Kids to Spout Coal Propoganda," Think Progress, February 14, 2008. www.thinkprogress.org.

Ryan Gilbey
: "Directors Who Exploit Children Should Collapse Out of Shame," *Guardian* (United Kingdom), July 15, 2008. www.guardian.co.uk.

Jordana Lewis
: "Minor Contracts, Major Issues: Inside the Coogan Act," *Hollywood Reporter*, March 5, 2007.

Jeffrey M. McCall
: "TV Exploits Children in 'Reality' Shows That Put Ratings First," *Atlanta Journal-Constitution*, June 4, 2009.

Dean Nelson and Barney Henderson
: "*Slumdog* Child Stars Miss Out on Movie Millions," *Telegraph* (United Kingdom), January 26, 2009.

Susan Parker
: "If You Mean It, Don't Exploit Children," *Berkeley Daily Planet*, January 29, 2008.

Peter Sanders
: "Disney Revs Up Tween Star Machine," *Wall Street Journal*, June 17, 2008.

CHAPTER 4

What Role Do Parents Play in Their Children's Careers in Entertainment?

Chapter Preface

Gypsy is one of the most critically acclaimed and popular Broadway musicals in the American canon. It is notable for its songs, but also for the character of Rose, a complexly written stage mother who pushes her two young daughters into vaudeville careers and then her oldest daughter into a life as a burlesque stripper. By the end of the show, she admits that she was motivated by her personal desire for fame rather than her children's desires to choose the course of their own lives. This characterization of Rose is based on the portrayal of her real-life counterpart, Rose Thompson Hovick, in her daughter Gypsy Rose Lee's widely read memoir—a story written from the child performer's point of view.

Parents have the responsibility to prepare their children for successful adult lives, and most parents try to help their children identify their particular talents and develop them into skills and interests that will serve them in the future, while still tending to their present childhood needs. This balance can be difficult to find in some instances, like when a child manifests extraordinary talent for performing (or attracts the attention of an interested producer) and starts earning money as a model, actor, or musical performer. These parents have to decide how much stress and pressure their children can handle, whether short-term sacrifices are likely to turn into long-term gains, if their children really enjoy public exposure, and—in some cases—what to do with any earnings.

Because many unscrupulous parents have taken complete advantage of their children's earning power, laws have been enacted that address how much time a child can spend acting, how much academic schooling a child is required to receive each day, how much of a child's wages a parent can spend and how much a parent must save, and how rigorously children can be held to signed contracts regarding their performances.

The California Child Actor's Bill, known as the Coogan Bill, is the most famous of these; it is named after Jackie Coogan, who earned millions of dollars as a child film actor in the 1920s, but received only $126,000 of it after his mother and stepfather spent it all on luxury items while he was working. The law was enacted in 1939 and was updated in 2004 to require employers to pay part of a child's wages directly to a trust fund and to stipulate that 100 percent of the money earned belongs to the child, and that parents who use the money without authorization are stealing it.

Lost income is not the only danger facing child actors. Performing is highly demanding work, and the stress of it— even for children who enjoy it—takes its toll. Although the curse of the child star that turns into a dysfunctional adult is mostly myth, there are spectacular examples of famous children who grew up to be self-destructive. Parents need to know when to nudge a reluctant child to work a little harder, when to take a break for school or for rest, and when to call it quits. Parents also need to know when to let a director take control of a child and when to intervene on the child's behalf as well as how to choose a manager or agent, negotiate a contract, step in and out of the spotlight, and take care of and nurture the talents of siblings, too. It is a complicated situation, but very often also a rewarding and happy one.

The following chapter investigates some of the ways that parents help or hinder their budding and working child performers, and how the particular characteristics of the entertainment industry affect all the members of a show business family.

> "It falls to mom and dad to routinely ask, 'Is this production company doing the right thing by my child?'"

Parents Should Be Involved in Their Children's Performance Careers

Ryan Thomas

Ryan Thomas has written several articles for Back Stage: The Actor's Resource, an organization that publishes a newsletter and hosts a Web site to provide actors with resources they need to participate in theater communities nationwide. The following viewpoint addresses an audience of "stage parents," people trying to strike a balance between the personal needs of their children and accommodating the requests of movie and theater producers who want young actors to work beyond the legal limits. Thomas explains that parents must be present to be advocates for their children.

Ryan Thomas, "Sing Out, Louise?: How Can Parents of Young Performers Balance Good Business and Competent Child Rearing?" Back Stage: The Actor's Resource, October 17, 2006. Copyright © 2006 VNU Business Media, Inc. All rights reserved. Reproduced by permission.

As you read, consider the following questions:

1. According to the author, why do parents walk a fine line between protecting their children from being exploited by studios and ensuring that their children are sought-after actors?

2. What is the difference between the legal emancipation of minors and the educational emancipation of minors, as explained in the viewpoint?

3. As described by the author, how has the Internet made the matter of protecting a child's image more important than in earlier decades?

For young performers, acting has all the allure of a grand new adventure. It's an entrance into a world of dress-up and make-believe, of working with grownups, earning money, and maybe—if fortune smiles upon them—seeing themselves on television or onscreen at the multiplex. For parents of young performers, some of those rewards apply, but they come hand in hand with other pressures: questions about contracts and legal affairs, as well as concerns about how much a child can and should endure, and what work is appropriate.

Hollywood has historically painted stage parents—mothers in particular—as meddling monsters, frustrated Mama Rose [a character from the musical *Gypsy*] types who would exploit their children to secure the fame the parents never experienced. The reality, of course, is quite different. It falls to mom and dad to routinely ask, "Is this production company doing right by my child? Am I doing right by my child? Or by the rest of the family that has been uprooted or separated to make this dream a reality?"

This business is, to put it mildly, a killer for actor and parent. "You're kind of squeezed. You want to please everybody," says Judy Savage of the Savage Agency. "Just that very word, 'stage parent': You're automatically despised the moment you walk on the set. You really have to walk that middle road, and I think there's a lot of pressure."

"Everything about being a parent in this business comes with pressure and uncertainty, and the pressure you put on yourself is very difficult," agrees Paula Dorn, cofounder of the watchdog and advocacy group [the] BizParentz [Foundation], and the mother of 16-year-old actor Patrick Dorn. "On top of that, we're completely maligned. Everyone hates a stage parent."

Knowledge Is Power

The general consensus among parents of young actors, especially parents who have had dealings in the industry before their child broke in, is that old adage about knowledge equating to power: The more you know, the better prepared you'll be to face the challenges. And like-minded representation from a conscientious agent or manager can be invaluable.

Though their kids may end up vying for the same roles at auditions, parents of acting children have been known to bond, formally and informally, to swap information and hash out industry issues that arise. Organizations such as the Screen Actors Guild [SAG] Young Performers Committee and Biz-Parentz exist to help parents of young performers walk an easier path. Good old-fashioned parental radar counts for a lot, too. If a request made of your child feels somehow off, ask questions, and keep asking until you're satisfied. And be prepared to chuck the project altogether.

It's no easy road, no matter how successful a child actor is or how much confidence his or her parents bring to the table. The family that pulls up stakes and moves starry-eyed to Los Angeles with dreams that the child will be the next Frankie Muniz or Lindsay Lohan may not know that those people peddling headshots and classes in the mall don't necessarily hold the key to stardom. Or that there are strict labor laws about how many hours per day a minor can legally work, what kind of schooling is required, and how much supervision is required on a set.

Achieving the Right Balance

Mothers and fathers of child actors will always face pressure—to have their child work a few more hours or stick around for another few takes, confront riskier material, or investigate legal emancipation—all in the name of forging good relationships, career advancement, or simply gaining an edge. Never mind those who would ask parents to consider the consequences to their child's career if they make the "wrong" decision and upset the wrong people.

Be a true Mama Rose, however, and you risk killing your child's career entirely. "We're still parents, and it's still our job to raise happy, normal children who will go on and be successful in life," says Dorn. "Parents are not all evil and stupid, and nobody should be telling you what you should do. But how would a parent know?" The answer? By doing your homework, or by relying on competent representation to do that homework for you.

"There's definitely a learning curve for parent and child," says Justin Shenkarow, national chairman of the SAG Young Performers Committee. "If a sibling of a child has been in the business, then the parents know right away; but if they're moving in from another state, it can be overwhelming trying to figure out the process of how things go." Like some of his fellow committee members, Shenkarow is a former child star; he played eldest son Matthew Brock on TV's *Picket Fences*. Other committee members are parents of young actors. "It often takes a year and sometimes longer for a parent to fully understand, sometimes longer and sometimes shorter depending on the parent," adds Shenkarow. "We encourage people to come to SAG seminars, go to auditioning agents, ask the right questions, and gain as much knowledge as possible." . . .

Labor Law Lessons

The negotiation of work hours is one of the main issues faced by young performers and their parents. By law, school-age children under 18, with the exception of those who have graduated from high school, are permitted to work only a limited number of hours per day. Schooling hours and mandated rest and recreation breaks are factored in.

California laws governing minors in the entertainment industry are, advocates note, among the strictest in the United States. A child between ages nine and 15 is allowed to work only five hours on a school day, and parents are within their legal rights to blow the whistle once little Timmy or Susie has reached that threshold. But the slope gets slippery when the light is fading, the work isn't complete, and the producers of a low-budget movie don't have the cash to crank the same set up anew the following day. If the child clearly isn't exhausted, they might argue, what's an extra 15 minutes of work time? An extra hour? "It's tricky. You can set a precedent, and anything you give, they'll take," says Eileen Mumy, whose daughter Liliana, age 12, appeared in both *Cheaper by the Dozen* movies and will be seen in *The Santa Clause 3.* "So I think you have to be very clear about, 'She's done. Goodbye. We'll see you tomorrow.'" Mumy, a member of the SAG Young Performers Committee, also acknowledges that common sense sometimes has to prevail. If a child has a regular or recurring role on a TV series, and the parents have a strong relationship with the producers, enough trust should exist to indicate that an extra 10 or 15 minutes does not signal a producer or director looking to take unfair advantage.

Anne Henry, BizParentz cofounder with Dorn, says producers routinely schedule close-up shots of children toward the end of the workday, figuring that most parents will stick around rather than forgo their child's "money shot." Henry, who has two children in the business and a third who acted as a child and has retired, has learned how to play the negotiating game. With 45 minutes left in the workday, she reminds the on-set teacher or welfare worker that the clock is ticking. When the request for an additional 15 minutes comes, as it invariably does, Henry agrees to be a team player. After those 15 minutes are up, she informs the person making the request, she'll take her child and leave whether the shot is complete or not. "I'm the one with the talent. I'm the one with the power. I've got the kids, and I can walk away," says Henry. "There's strength in knowing how this game is played versus acting stupid and clueless. Give them the extra 15 minutes and then you leave." . . .

Between Eileen Mumy's SAG work and the fact that Liliana's father, Bill, was a child star—he played Will Robinson on TV's *Lost in Space*—the Mumy family knows how to handle pressure. Liliana was recently called to audition for a TV show. The decision to turn it down came not from the parents but from Liliana. "She said, 'Those dates are homecoming, and I'm not missing homecoming,'" her mother says. "Homecoming is more important to her than a TV show."

Legal vs. Educational Emancipation

The closer young actors come to graduation day, the more likely it is they will hear the word "emancipation," particularly those actors who have a prospering career. Kids wish they were old enough to work as much as they liked without the interference of chemistry tests? Well, they can divorce themselves from their parents and that freedom is theirs—or so the temptation goes. How many more roles might they be up for if, as emancipated minors, they could beat out the 19-year-old who looks young?

Though well-known actors, such as Jena Malone and Macaulay Culkin, have successfully emancipated themselves, Dorn and most of the parents interviewed for this article agreed that such a move should be a last resort. Even the terminology is misleading, says Henry, adding that casting direc-

Denise Jonas Talks About Parenting the Jonas Brothers

"It's important for parents not to be afraid of their kids' talents," Denise says. "I know parents with multiple children who don't feel it's equitable across the board to assist one child. But I say, 'Go for it.'" Because in Denise's experience, celebrating individual gifts helps everyone find his best place. . . .

Denise had few concerns about her boys missing the usual activities of childhood, like soccer practice. "I did not think about the negative aspects of stage life or being child stars. We simply thought about the responsibility we'd carry." Success came quickly to the Jonases, but not without a taste of failure: In 2006, their first record label, Columbia, dropped the group, reportedly telling Team Jonas, "The [success] indicators aren't there."

While their dad has described the band's rejection by the label as "devastating," the boys just say the experience provided important perspective on the blessings they enjoy today. Whatever they suffered, they suffered it extraordinarily quickly. Hollywood Records signed them up, and their next album, *Jonas Brothers*—supported by slickly produced videos—went double-platinum, selling nearly three million copies worldwide.

Amanda Robb, "How to Raise Rock Stars,"
Good Housekeeping, *July 2009.*

tors who send out breakdowns for "emancipated minors only" are looking for an actor who has fulfilled the educational requirements to work as an adult, not someone who has petitioned the court to be legally emancipated. Jennifer Jines, whose daughter Courtney recently turned 14, says, "Interestingly enough, I just had that conversation with her manager. I said, 'Don't even ask me. It's not happening. She's going to finish high school.'" Adds Jane Gordon, whose 15-year-old son, Jonah Meyerson, appeared in *The Royal Tenenbaums* and TV's *The Book of Daniel*, "My son is a really terrific student; he goes to a civilian school that's not filled with actors, and it's a very competitive academic program. We're unwilling to sacrifice his education for work. Fortunately his agent supports us on that."

A better option, Dorn says, is to have a young performer who has reached age 16 or the second semester of his or her sophomore year take the California High School Proficiency Exam [CHSPE], administered twice a year. Young performers who pass that test can work adult hours and still take high school classes or community college classes for college credit. The CHSPE was designed not specifically for the entertainment industry but rather for children who have to work to contribute to the family's income. Dorn says, "It works well for us, and we hope they never take it away. You get the best of both worlds, and you can satisfy what the production needs without going through the emotionally ugly scenario of a legal emancipation." . . .

Protecting a Child's Image in the Present and Future

The Internet has created a haven for pedophiles and sexual predators to track a young performer's career with the same enthusiasm of any fan. Given the ability of people to do screen captures of film or TV scenes on their computers, any visual image can become immortalized and end up on someone's wall. The idea that an image of their son shirtless, smoking, or engaged in provocative behavior can trail him indefinitely on the Web should prompt parents to be extra careful about the kind of work they let their child do.

According to BizParentz, the ease of screen capture and the increase in predatory activity coincided—perhaps not so coincidentally—with the changing nature and quality of roles called for in scripts. We've reached a point where the agent of busy child star Dakota Fanning talks early Oscar buzz for the 12-year-old's performance in the upcoming feature *Hounddog*, for which Fanning filmed child rape scenes and reportedly appeared partially naked.

Henry said her son nixed the chance to audition for a movie in which his character would have to do a pole dance in Victoria's Secret lingerie for Lindsay Lohan. Henry didn't even tell him about the low-budget film that involved portrayals of pedophilia, sex between boys, and one boy getting hit with a baseball bat while sexually servicing another boy. "Now I feel that if I make a mistake in choosing a role, it could be on the Internet forever. My kid's kids are going to deal with it," says Henry, whose daughter Jillian, age 9, is also an actor. "I'll read on message boards about casting, and it will be, 'Oh, my God, no way in hell is my kid doing that,' and other parents will say, 'Well, maybe. Who's casting it?'" If it sounds like a parent is choosing to manage her child's entertainment-industry career the way a CEO runs a business, well, that's kind of what's required. With experience comes wisdom and a more finely honed scam radar that can help override outside pressures from people saying, "You must do this."

> *"It's hard, but it's what Corey wants. . . .*
> *If it was any of my children, I'd make*
> *the same sacrifice."*

Parents Often Make Serious Sacrifices to Further Their Children's Careers

Paul Grondahl

Paul Grondahl has been a staff writer for the Times Union *newspaper in Albany since 1984, where he has covered news and features and won several awards for his journalism work. He is also the author of several books on historical and political topics. The following viewpoint highlights some of the steps parents in New York have taken to help their minor children pursue careers as actors or dancers on Broadway. Many of these people split up families and quit jobs to move to New York City with the performing child to be closer to the theaters and avoid long, daily commutes.*

As you read, consider the following questions:

1. As cited by Grondahl, what is the minimum weekly sum a child will earn in a Broadway production?

2. As noted in the viewpoint, how many minutes is Jacob Clemente on stage for each performance of *Gypsy*?

3. What are the other children in the Clemente family doing while Jacob performs in New York City, as explained by Grondahl?

Four local kids who rode their training at Eleanor's School of Dance on Central Avenue to the bright lights of Broadway have achieved at a tender age a dream many adult performers never attain.

But for their parents and siblings, the logistics can be nightmarish: a divided family, grueling commutes, sky-high Manhattan rents, sacrificing one parental income, homeschooling demands and the strain of eight performances a week on an adolescent.

Ah, show biz.

"It's not for everybody that young. Basically, they're giving up their childhoods," said Eleanor Leonardi, the school's proprietor and longtime dance teacher.

She warns parents whose children have displayed great talent while still wearing braces to be careful what they wish for, even if the payoff includes an Actors' Equity minimum weekly paycheck of about $1,500.

"Show business is not an easy road," she said.

Then again, being on Broadway has given these kids a career boost and glimpses of a world they could hardly imagine, such as getting to meet Elton John, Hillary Rodham Clinton, Robert De Niro, Liza Minnelli and the cast of *High School Musical*.

One Family Split Across Two Cities

Corey Snide, 15, enrolled as a sophomore at Colonie High School, is starring in the Broadway musical *13*, about the drama and loathing of middle school cliques. He previously danced the title role in the London stage production of *Billy Elliot*.

His early success has come at a high cost to his family. His mom quit her job selling dance supplies at Eleanor's School of Dance and moved into an apartment with her son in Jersey City, N.J. Her husband, Ron, who works in construction, drives down on weekends with their 10-year-old child while maintaining their Colonie home. They also have two college-aged children.

"It's hard, but it's what Corey wants," said his mom, Johnna Snide. "If it was any of my children, I'd make the same sacrifice."

In addition to homeschooling her son, she accompanies him each day to the Bernard B. Jacobs Theatre on West 45th Street for his performance in *13*, which features an all-teenage cast and onstage teen band. Despite some good reviews, it struggled to fill seats during the week and will close Jan. 4 [2009] after just 105 performances. It joins other abbreviated runs and Broadway theaters going dark in the wake of the economic recession.

Now, with an apartment lease, a home mortgage, just one income and an uncertain future for their son's budding career, the Snides are pondering their next move.

"We don't have any regrets at all," Johnna Snide said. "If your kid loves this as much as Corey does, you have to back their dreams."

For now, they're staying put so Corey can continue to audition in New York. A representative from Nickelodeon, the popular kids' cable TV network, recently met with Corey.

Economically, the family has taken a hit, although part of Corey's *13* salary goes to pay rent on the apartment and part goes into his savings and college tuition accounts. "He works hard for it," his mom said.

Linda Septien's Simple Rules for Becoming a Pop Star

Rule No. 3: Don't be an orphan.

Deborah Dingwall, the chatty, outgoing mom of Annie and Caroline, has driven 800 miles this week, carting her kids around with the incredible energy of a woman who has nothing else on her mind but making sure her offspring get exactly what they want. Right now, that means 20 or 30 hours of extracurricular activities a week.

Weekdays, Annie has to be carried from the Dingwall home in Plano [Texas] to Oak Cliff, where she attends Booker T. Washington High School for the Performing [and Visual] Arts. Then, Caroline must be dropped off back at her private school in the northern suburbs. After that, it's a juggling act between basketball practices, dance classes and flying up and down the tollway to Addison Circle and the Septien Vocal Studio. Somewhere in there, Dingwall's teenage son has to be dealt with. But despite a few reservations about her kids' ride on the fast track to fame, Dingwall is dedicated to helping them along the way.

"If that's what you want, let's find a way to do it," Dingwall says she told her kids when they expressed an interest in music. Annie started out in group lessons with other teachers at the studio before being invited to audition for the master class. The program isn't for the casual user; kids spend hours each week in acting, songwriting and instrumentation lessons as well as voice. If they have other interests, as Annie does with 12 hours a week of ballet classes or Caroline with after-school athletics, those things get squeezed in the spaces in between.

Andrea Grimes, "Star Factory," Dallas Observer, March 2, 2006.

Another Family Split Apart

Jude and Linda Clemente of North Greenbush [New York] trade off with each other midweek, staying in the $2,000-a-month one-bedroom apartment in Midtown Manhattan with their 11-year-old son, Jacob, a sixth grader at Goff Middle School. He performs in the *Gypsy* ensemble as a Boy Scout at the St. James Theatre on West 44th Street. Jacob's highlight is singing a one-note solo in the first act and he's on stage for less than 25 minutes.

On Sunday evening, after the show, they drive back home so Jacob can spend Monday, Broadway's dark day, with his three adolescent siblings for a touch of normalcy. One of his parents drives back Monday night and they repeat the drill.

"It's hectic and crazy, but Jacob loves it and it's been a fun experience for all of us," said his mother, a lawyer, who had to scale back the billable hours at her private legal practice. Her husband, president of Troy Sand & Gravel, also has made sacrifices on his work schedule.

The Clementes have logged more than, 35,000 miles on a 2008 Town & Country minivan purchased in March [2008]. On top of Jacob's crowded Broadway schedule, the other Clemente kids take dance classes at Eleanor's and Myers Ballet School in Schenectady. They also performed in the *Nutcracker* at Proctor's and at a holiday show in East Greenbush, and one is in rehearsal for *Rent* at the Cohoes Music Hall.

The family will get an early reprieve from their thruway grind when the Patti LuPone revival about stripper Gypsy Rose Lee and her indomitable mother closes on Jan. 11 [2009], after 332 performances. That's two months earlier than planned, due to anemic ticket sales.

The Clementes' landlord, an understanding sort who's in the performing arts, is letting them out of their apartment lease early.

"My heart isn't breaking that we don't have to make that drive every week," said Linda Clemente, who will continue to homeschool her son when they return to North Greenbush. He is now being represented by agent Nancy Carson and the family will weigh carefully future opportunities for Jacob.

Maintaining an Almost-Cohesion

Both Lisa and Keith Fragomeni of Guilderland [New York] picked up the pace in their lives so their daughter Brianna, 12, a seventh grader at Farnsworth Middle School, could make her Broadway debut as an ensemble ballet girl in *Billy Elliot*. The hit musical is at the Imperial Theatre on West 45th Street and a long run is anticipated.

Keith Fragomeni works for the state thruway and drives to New York City on weekends to be with his wife and daughter. They share a two-bedroom apartment on Roosevelt Island with a family friend. The couple also has a son in college.

"It's difficult, but we're managing," said Lisa Fragomeni, who scaled back her job working banquets at the Marriott on Wolf Road. "It's doing so much for my daughter and she loves it. We'd do it again in a second."

She's given up some income to stay with her daughter, but they've established a bank account for Brianna that she can access when she turns 18.

Another Eleanor's School of Dance alum, Marina Micalizzi, 14, also is a ballet girl in *Billy Elliot*.

Her family found a solution to the commuting dilemma: They moved from Clifton Park [New York] to New York City.

| *"These teenagers are the winners of Hollywood's gene-pool lottery."*

Celebrity Parents Can Nurture Their Children's Fame

Chris Ayres

Chris Ayres is the Los Angeles correspondent for the Times *of* London *and the author of* War Reporting for Cowards, *a critically acclaimed account of the war in Iraq. He was nominated as Foreign Correspondent of the Year in 2004. The following viewpoint looks at the common occurrence of celebrity parents who help their children establish their own Hollywood careers. Ayres says these children are known as the SADOs: sons and daughters of . . . (stars). He notes their critics decry Hollywood nepotism, but their defenders point out that children in many industries follow in their parents' footsteps.*

As you read, consider the following questions:

1. How does Andrew Breitbart support his argument that Hollywood is not a meritocracy, according to Ayres?

2. What conflict does Jeff Bridges feel about how fame is used in his family, as cited by the author?

3. According to the viewpoint, what anxieties do some SADOs experience after being settled into an entertainment career with a parent's help?

It is almost midnight in Beverly Hills. Outside the extraterrestrial-looking Prada boutique on Rodeo Drive, the 20-year-old actress Lindsay Lohan is twirling and air-kissing under the heat of several dozen flashbulbs. A line of black T-shirted valets welcomes the Aston Martins and Maybachs as they pull up outside the party. Standing behind the black velvet rope is the well-known nightlife correspondent for a newswire service.

"Who the hell are these people?" she complains, as yet another flock of teenagers, all bad hair and preppy blazers, climb awkwardly from a car the price of a Venice Beach apartment. "They look as though they should have been put to bed at least an hour ago."

The correct question is not "Who are these people?" but "Who are their parents?"—for these teenagers are the winners of Hollywood's gene-pool lottery: the product of every on-set romance in deepest NmubuOoboo, every ill-advised quickie in the Club World bathroom, and every between-take latte with the key grip's daughter.

If the members of this Hollywood über-class had a catchy, media-friendly acronym (they don't, but I'm willing to offer one), they would be the SADOs: the "sons and daughters of . . ."

All of which matters little—an invitation to join Mary-Kate Olsen in the smoking section of a Prada party is hardly consolation for the blight of celebrity parents—until they get a job in Hollywood. And then the world sees green. Consider the reaction of the British tabloid press to photographs of 16-year-old Lorraine Nicholson out on the town with her 69-year-old movie star father, Jack Nicholson. "Jack the lad out with a teenage blonde!" sneered the *Mail*, noting with palpable distaste that the snaps with daddy could only help Lorrie's acting career (she has a cameo in the widely derided Adam Sandler blockbuster *Click*).

But how prevalent is nepotism in Hollywood? And does it matter? Should we care that Tori Spelling is Aaron Spelling's daughter; that Sofia Coppola's dad directed *The Godfather*, or that Liv Tyler was going to Aerosmith concerts before she was going to pre-school? Haven't Jeff Bridges and Nicolas Cage proved themselves enough to end the jibes about their A-list relatives (in case you're wondering, Cage is part of the Coppola clan). How much more money does Ben Stiller have to make—and how many more on-screen credits must he give himself (he managed six for *Zoolander*) before he is more than Jerry Stiller's boy?

Do Children of Celebrities Deserve Their Fame?

I put this question to Andrew Breitbart, professional trouble-maker for the news Web site the Drudge Report and coauthor of the anti-celebrity tirade *Hollywood, Interrupted*. He begins to hyperventilate almost immediately. "Someone like Tori Spelling is the average girl on the street," he rages. "Yet she's cast as one of the good-looking chicks in *Beverly Hills, 90210* and we're not supposed to notice? Clearly, Hollywood is not a meritocracy. There are no checks and balances against nepotism that, in any other industry, would result in people rolling their eyes. Can you imagine being told at the hospital: 'Actually, Dr McDonald's son is going to perform this surgery today'? In just about every industry less sexy than Hollywood there are rules against this kind of thing."

Breitbart makes a strong case, but isn't this just the ranting of an embittered outsider? What do those who actually work in the business think? I call an A-list screenwriter who would rather lose a kidney than be named in a *Times* article about nepotism.

Squirming, he offers this. "Nepotism is a lot like narcissism in Hollywood. It's so pervasive, it's actually hard to identify." He cites under-the-radar examples such as Christian Slater, whose mother is the legendary casting agent Mary Jo Slater (Ms Slater did not return my call, thus no light was shed on her role in her son's acting success). Yet family is not the only enemy of equal opportunity, he says. Many stars, such as Adam Sandler, tend to employ only their closest buddies. In one possibly apocryphal incident, an A-list actor even insisted on casting his own horse.

To Susan Jansen, who created the hit television show and movie *Lizzie McGuire* (which helped to launch the megabrand that is Hilary Duff), no one should be ashamed of the N-word. Unlike many in Hollywood, she concedes openly that her first break was the result of family contacts. "I'd just gotten out of film school," she remembers. "My mom had been talking to my uncle Howard about how miserable I was, so he called me up and said 'do you want to write comedy? It's a nice life'. Uncle Howard was a business affairs lawyer for Paramount, and he did things like negotiate the contracts for *Cheers*. Anyway, uncle Howard got me a meeting with the head of TV at Paramount—a meeting I probably wouldn't even be able to get today."

Not that the meeting with Mr Paramount went smoothly. Says Jansen: "We sat down and he asked me what TV shows I liked. I told the truth: I didn't watch TV, I didn't own a TV and I grew up without a TV. He looked at me like I was the biggest idiot who ever walked the planet. But I was there because of Uncle Howard, so he said 'Why don't you go out, buy a TV, watch some of our shows and, if you feel like it, you can write a script for me.'"

Four days later, she did just that. The *Lizzie McGuire Movie* alone went on to make almost $60 million (£33 million). These days Jansen lives in Bel Air, in the former estate of the aviation pioneer Howard Hughes.

Of course, Jansen would never have achieved so much without her considerable talent. The same can be said of Jeff Bridges, who landed his first movie role at the age of six months (his father was Lloyd Bridges, the blond heartthrob star of the long-running television series *Sea Hunt*). Nevertheless, the knowledge that so many beneficiaries of nepotism are unburdened by ability can result in paranoia.

In a recent profile interview for the *Times*, Bridges told me that he was still bothered by his father's early help. "I'm a product of nepotism," he said. "The doors were open to me. I'd done several movies before I decided what I wanted to do. There was a certain amount of guilt about whether I really had what it takes."

Should Parents Use Their Celebrity to Help Their Children?

As a result, Bridges refused to groom his daughters. "I thought I'd be less proactive," he said. "One of the hardest things for an actor is getting your first break. Now (my daughters) are in their twenties, they're leaving college, moving out of the house and looking for careers. I'm thinking 'Jeez, maybe I should have encouraged them more.'"

None of this is new to Dr Jenn Berman, a Beverly Hills psychotherapist whose clients have included several SADOs. "When someone is successful and their parents are also successful, the kind of question that comes up is, 'Do people think I got this job just because of my dad?'" she says. "That can be a very big one to overcome."

According to Dr Berman, the temperament of the famous parent is key: "If they are absent or difficult, or just don't know how to be a parent, then in their children you tend to see drug and alcohol abuse, depression, anxiety, eating disorders and, in really terrible cases, suicide."

But can't the same be said of ordinary families? Yes, says Dr Berman, but the wealth of A-list households makes a big difference. "Instead of being able to afford a bit of marijuana, they can afford a whole lot of cocaine," she says. "Instead of not wearing a helmet and falling off their skateboard, they don't wear a seatbelt and crash their parents' Ferrari."

Indeed, there is an entire subgenre of journalism dedicated to chronicling the misfortunes of such celebrity offspring as Chris Brosnan (adopted son of the former 007 Pierce), who was arrested last year [2005] for heroin possession after a police chase through South London. On emerging from an epic stint in rehab, Brosnan Jr found work—directing a film. "Dad's not involved but I'd love to work with him one day," he told the *News of the World*. "I just want to make him proud."

More tragic was the death of Chris Penn, son of the director Leo Penn and younger brother of Sean. Unlike his father and brother, Penn managed only supporting roles such as Nice Guy Eddie in *Reservoir Dogs*; by the time of his death this year he weighed 300 lbs. and had a long history of drug abuse. The postmortem examination suggested that death was from natural causes.

Of course, many SADOs don't even try to compete with their parents. Says Dr Berman: "Some children of celebrities feel that they'll never be as successful as their mom or dad, no matter what they do—a 'why bother trying' mentality. They struggle to find their own identity."

The Secondary Benefits of Celebrity Parenting

Yet such fame-addled products of Hollywood can still benefit from a different kind of nepotism: the best-selling memoir *Take*, for example, Christina Crawford's *Mommie Dearest*, or the late Gary Crosby's *Going My Own Way*, which offered horrifying accounts of the dysfunctional family lives of Joan Crawford and Bing Crosby respectively. The latter was perhaps the most extraordinary: Two of Bing's children, Lindsay and Dennis, committed suicide, with Lindsay reportedly taking his life the day after watching his father sing "White Christmas" on television. Both brothers were living on small allowances from their father's trust fund, and both died from self-inflicted gunshot wounds to the head.

With all this in mind, perhaps it's surprising that we don't pity the SADOs rather than begrudging them their genetic advantage at Hollywood job interviews. Yet at the same time no one wants to pay good money to watch a movie such as *Boxing Helena*, the amputation romance written and directed by one Jennifer Chambers Lynch, the wife of . . . well, you can probably guess.

The movie was so unspeakably awful (plot: boy meets girl, boy amputates girl's limbs one by one) that Kim Basinger backed out of an agreement to play the lead role, resulting in a successful $8.1 million lawsuit. The ruling was later overturned on appeal, with Basinger reaching an out-of-court deal.

Nepotism Is Just Part of Life

Andrew Breitbart says it is the press's duty to defend cinemagoers from the worst cases of nepotism, though he has little faith in the likes of *Variety* and *Vanity Fair* fulfilling it. "The bottom line in Hollywood is that everybody wants a deal," he says. "Even the journalists who write about Hollywood are trying to work out if this is a person who, one day, might want to read their script."

But the Internet is beginning to pick up the slack: There is already a site entitled The Hollywood Nepotism Page, which lists the likes of Jim Hanks, Daniel Baldwin, Dedee Pfeiffer and Donal Gibson.

Back at the Prada party, I watch the SADOs as they walk up in turn to Dustin Hoffman and slap him on the back (a friend of dad's, no doubt), but I can't feel much jealousy: These teenagers might drive Porsche convertibles in high school but they'll spend their lives being ridiculed if they make it and ridiculed if they don't.

As for their parents, why should we be so shocked when they try to build a dynasty? The Bushes did it, as did the descendants of Henry Ford. Yet in Hollywood, empire-building always provokes more outrage.

Susan Jansen says that we need to move on—nepotism is just part of the survival instinct: "Where's the surprise? Here is a good job that is overpaid for the amount of labour involved, so you want to hand it over as a favour to someone you know. Why on earth wouldn't you? The point of nepotism is that you want to get that favour back at some point. You want to be able to call someone and say, 'Hey, you owe me.'"

> *"From infancy ... mother and grand-*
> *mother told the angelically pretty little*
> *girl that she would be bigger than*
> *Marilyn Monroe."*

Celebrity Parents Can Exploit Their Children's Fame

Judith Newman

Judith Newman writes a monthly column for Ladies' Home Journal *and is a contributing editor for* Allure *and* Self. *She also writes for* Vanity Fair, Harper's, Discover, *and the* New York Times. *In the following viewpoint, Newman examines how Paris Hilton's mother and grandmother pushed her into the spotlight to cash in personally on her fame and notoriety. Newman acknowledges speculation about how much money the Hiltons really have and questions the family's motives.*

As you read, consider the following questions:

1. What was baby Paris Hilton's first nickname, as noted by Newman?

2. According to Newman, how did Kathy and Rick Hilton personally benefit from the reality television show *I Want to Be a Hilton*?

3. How much money were the Hiltons paid by NBC to give an interview about Paris Hilton's jail time, as cited by Newman?

There are plenty of stars whose mothers are their constant companions and succor; Justin Timberlake and Leo DiCaprio, to name two, escort their moms to big events all the time. But they don't make good copy. More intriguing are the parents who seem hell-bent on helping their children realize their dreams. But what dreams? And whose?

If ever there was a woman to make [American burlesque entertainer and actress] Gypsy Rose Lee look shy and unassuming, it's Kathleen Elizabeth Avanzino Richards Hilton. Hilton was herself the daughter of a stage mother, the pretty, vivacious Kathy Dugan, known to everyone as Big Kathy. Dugan, writes Jerry Oppenheimer in his 2006 book, *House of Hilton*, was an Irish Catholic high school dropout who grew up in Manhasset, Long Island, eventually marrying four times. She told her daughters again and again that marrying rich wasn't a goal; it was the goal.

From the time Big Kathy's children were infants, they were in the spotlight. Little Kathy was only a small child when she started modeling. Eventually Big Kathy moved to L.A. to help boost her daughters' careers. While sisters Kim Richards and Kyle Richards are working as actresses today (Kyle in frequent TV gigs and Kim most recently as Christina Ricci's mother in *Black Snake Moan*), Big Kathy's namesake snared only a few bit parts, on shows such as *The Rockford Files* and *Happy Days*. "Of course Kathy wanted to be a star," says Hollywood party cougar and Hilton friend Nikki Haskell. "Who didn't?"

Kathy never got her big break, but she did find her Prince Charming. According to Oppenheimer, she had known Ricky Hilton—the sixth child of eight born to Barron Hilton—since they were teenagers, and they began dating seriously in 1978. Rick was a sweet University of Denver party boy. (Not that the entrepreneurial Hilton spirit was dead within him: He was known for throwing fabulous parties at the Denver Hilton and charging students 20 bucks a head.) Soon he was smitten with Kathy, and the two were married in Beverly Hills on November 24, 1979. They have, by all accounts, a very loving marriage (Rick is known to call his wife "Mommy," the *New York Post* noted in 2005), though whether that love is shared by the extended Hilton family is questionable.

In 1981, Kathy had Paris, whom she nicknamed "Star." From infancy, says Oppenheimer, mother and grandmother told the angelically pretty little girl that she would be bigger than Marilyn Monroe, bigger than Princess Di. All she needed was a little boost. (Kathy Hilton did not respond to *V.F.*'s [*Vanity Fair*'s] requests for comment.)

"After my research I came away with sympathy for Paris," says Oppenheimer. "When she was a kid she thought about becoming a veterinarian. But she had no chance to do anything but what she has done." (For her part, Paris once told a reporter that her professional dreams changed when she realized she "could just buy a bunch of animals.")

"Kathy and Rick would host parties at these little clubs in New York, where they'd hand out flyers—something like 'Young and Rich Party hosted by Nicky and Paris Hilton,'" says Suzan Hughes, who was married to Herbalife founder Mark Hughes and is godmother to Kathy's younger son, Conrad IV. "You throw a great party, you get a celeb to show up—or you say that a celeb will show up—and when the camera crews come the celeb may not be there, but there's your gorgeous daughter, dancing on a table. That's how it all began." . . .

The money really began to roll in. Paris's showing up and waving became a major source of income. Hilton gets paid anywhere from $50,000 to upwards of $150,000 to appear at an opening, says an executive who books stars for events. (This year [2007], he says, she got $150,000 to host her birthday party at the Hard Rock Hotel in Las Vegas.) Then there are the endorsements for lines of jewelry, makeup, and fragrance; the Club Paris nightclubs; and her reality show, *The Simple Life*, with fellow bad-girl-trying-to-turn-good Nicole Richie. The show was dropped in July; Hilton is reportedly in talks to star in an upcoming season of the British version of *Celebrity Big Brother*, where cameras and mikes follow your every move as you live in a house with a bunch of other famous people—which shouldn't be all that different from how she's living now, except that she'll be paid hundreds of thousands of dollars to do it for a few weeks.

The manna of stardom was not showered only on Paris. Her parents must be benefiting from her notoriety, and observers have begun to take note. "Take just one example," says Jerry Oppenheimer, "that horrible reality show *I Want to Be a Hilton*," where people vie for the chance to live the way Kathy Hilton thinks New York socialites do. (Fun fact: Upon arrival, contestants were taught the proper way to hold a wineglass—by the stem—and in the last scene everyone is holding the glass correctly, except Kathy Hilton.) "Kathy made a chunk of change as the host, and Rick was [a] producer." She is even staking a claim to the showing-up-and-waving business; right now, says the booking executive, she can bring in around $5,000 or $10,000 for an appearance.

More recently, Kathy signed a deal for her own skin care collection—"reflecting the luxurious Kathy Hilton lifestyle"—which she began selling on the Home Shopping Network on July 31. (While Kathy Hilton declined to be interviewed for this article, the publicist for the beauty products told me she could set us up, as long as I wrote exclusively about the beauty products.)

Such moneymaking endeavors seem almost ridiculous when compared with the vast Hilton fortune amassed by the hotel chain's founder, Paris's great-grandfather Conrad Hilton. Conrad believed in a strong work ethic (though he, like his

Hollywood Parents Help Their Kids—and Themselves

A boom in children's entertainment has created a new blood sport in Hollywood: show-business parents fighting to gain early access for their offspring to popular movies and television shows. Indeed, what admission to a private preschool is to some parents in New York, a trip backstage at *Hannah Montana* has become to certain moms and dads in Hollywood.

Crying, begging, bribing—executives at Nickelodeon, Disney Channel and Warner Bros. say they have seen it all.

To a 60-something star like Sylvester Stallone, getting his daughter onto the private *Hannah Montana* soundstage makes him not only an A-list parent, but also signals that he remains a member of Hollywood's ruling class. For big-shot agents, studio executives and producers, placing their children well within camera shot at the Nickelodeon Kids' Choice Awards is an insidery symbol of power.

Brooks Barnes, "The Littlest Big Shots,"
New York Times, *November 4, 2007.*

progeny, also enjoyed certain extravagances), and when he died, in 1979, he left his children and grandchildren relatively modest shares in the company. . . .

Rick Hilton does work for a living. (He co-owns Hilton & Hyland, a high-end real-estate business in L.A., which recently handled, among other deals, the sale of Paris's Spanish-style Hollywood Hills home for just under $4 million. His brother-in-law Mauricio Umansky—the husband of Kyle Richards, Kathy's sister—took care of the sale and pocketed the commission. Might as well keep it in the family.) But, for a family who has inherited wealth, the Hiltons have certainly picked up quite an assortment of odd jobs. Whatever money they have, it's hardly the vast fortune it appears to be.

"Listen, they don't have any real Hilton money there; Rick makes his money as a broker," says a friend and prominent New York real-estate developer. Anderson Cooper devoted an entire episode of his CNN show to a panel discussion of Paris's *Larry King Live* interview, and a good amount of time was spent discussing the question, "How much is the Hilton family really worth?" Cooper speculated, "I never believe people have as much money as they say or are portrayed on TV to have," and then invited *Forbes*'s Matthew Miller and others to rattle off a laundry list of Paris's independent enterprises.

The Hiltons' relatively modest means might explain "why they cultivate friends that have jets and yachts," adds another friend—who had a yacht. "They like to hitch rides." Her relationship with Kathy Hilton ended, the friend says, when she and her wealthy husband divorced. Kathy followed the wealthy husband, the new wife . . . and the money. Still, this friend and the Hiltons stayed in touch, until one memorable day about five years ago. "I went to Big Kathy's funeral—she'd died of breast cancer—and afterwards Rick and Kathy had people over to their house. Paris had just turned 21, and the Hiltons had a running loop of footage from Paris's 21st-birthday party up on their big-screen TV. Rick was running around going, 'Look at Paris!' It was a promotion."

One might argue, though, that, given her own ambition and sensibilities, Big Kathy would have been proud.

Further questions about the Hiltons' riches abound. For example, do very rich people commonly rent out their homes? The Hiltons have been renting out their seven-bedroom, seven-and-a-half-bath house in Southampton, New York, for years—this year, for approximately $350,000 for the summer. "He has money from his real-estate business, but it's nothing that can cover their lifestyle," says a wealthy New Yorker familiar with the Hiltons' housing situation. She has seen the house. She has heard this summer's renters are trying desperately to get some of the problems fixed. "Do I have to give you another $300,000 to get screens on the windows?" the tenant shouted, according to a mutual friend.

"Usually when people rent [out] a house for the summer, they clean it up," continues the woman. "This house was left exactly the way it was when the renters saw it in November. Everything in it is moldy and filthy. Most of the screens on the windows are broken. Their dogs are obviously not house-trained. But they don't see it. These are people whose daughter has sex on tape, and they think that's fine." (Kathy's friend Nikki Haskell, for her part, says Rick and Kathy are "adorable people," "diligent" parents who "love their children" and "want the best.")

And then there was the widely reported recent kerfuffle over Paris's post-jail interview. Barbara Walters and the Hiltons were doing the interview tango, seemingly successfully: Walters had known Kathy Hilton for years; Kathy and Nicky appeared at the celebration for Walters's star on the Hollywood Walk of Fame, and the Hiltons gave a party in her honor. The interview seemed to belong to Walters, but the Hiltons were being courted by other networks; Rick is said to have called Walters and told her NBC had made an offer—reportedly close to $1 million, which made ABC's $100,000 seem paltry. It was time for Walters and ABC to pony up.

One Hollywood publicist sees the squabbling over the interview as a betrayal of Walters by Kathy Hilton. "Not only was [Walters] furious at not getting the interview," the publicist says, citing a *Variety* article, "but she also knew how shabby it looked, letting it be known that the networks were paying for these interviews to begin with." The networks scuttled away from the project. Paris Hilton ultimately appeared for free on *Larry King Live*, where America learned that she had spent her jail time reading the Bible, but that she couldn't name her favorite passage. (Barbara Walters would say only, "Kathy seems to be a very nice lady who cares about her daughter.")

But why would people of still-considerable wealth care about being paid for an interview that (a) immediately makes them look morally suspect and (b) inevitably would make their poor daughter look mentally challenged? "Well, why not?" says columnist Lloyd Grove. "I mean, even if they are rich, money's money."

Periodical Bibliography

The following articles have been selected to supplement the diverse views presented in this chapter.

Julian Benbow   "Standing Out for Right, Wrong Reasons," *Boston Globe*, November 12, 2006.

Bharati Dubey   "Parents of Child Actors Happy with Their Work Conditions," *Times of India*, December 1, 2008.

Sean Hannity   "In New Film Child Actor Dakota Fanning Is Raped" (Interview Transcript), FOXNews.com, January 16, 2007.

Misty Harris   "Catwalks Rob Famous Cradles," Canwest News Service, September 5, 2009.

Peter Marks   "Child Actors Who Made Quite an Entrance," *Washington Post*, August 6, 2006.

Mireya Navarro   "Star Kids, Family Stress," *New York Times*, March 20, 2005.

Joal Ryan   "Attack of the Stage Parents!" E!Online, March 28, 2008.

Richard Shears   "My Fears for Little Miss Croc Hunter," *Daily Mail* (United Kingdom), November 19, 2007.

Randy Shore   "Child Actors: All Work and No Play," *Vancouver Sun*, August 10, 2009.

For Further Discussion

Chapter 1

1. Authors Rebecca Herr Stephenson and Sarah Banet-Weiser, and Jason C.G. Halford's team of authors all attribute to the entertainment industry an influence over children's diet. Children—especially very young children—are almost never able to procure their own food; it has to be brought into the home by adults. If children cannot choose what to eat, then, can entertainment directed at them really have any affect on their body weight or physical health? What factors really determine a child's body weight?

2. Ya-Lun Tsao identifies in youth books the propensity to perpetuate traditional gender stereotypes that define and limit what girls are "supposed" to do and look like. Nathalie op de Beeck acknowledges that conservative roles for males and females have changed for many, and presents evidence that a diversity of characters is available in children's publishing. Does it matter? Should a publishing company aim to please or mold its audience?

3. Boys and girls often compare themselves unfavorably to the unrealistic (and often doctored) images of the male and female ideal physical form, a situation linked to a range of psychological issues, from low self-esteem to eating disorders and steroid abuse. Is this a problem that can be solved? How does the idea that looks are more valuable than character get perpetuated? Should the media be held accountable for using these images? Should models have to conform to rules about minimum weight requirements?

Chapter 2

1. Jesse Walker claims that educational television programs for preschoolers, such as *Sesame Street*, have had a positive measurable effect on children's education. Caroline E. Mayer reports on a commercial, promotional company marketing to kids on the school bus, a captive audience of minors with little experience critically evaluating advertisements. Is the risk of taking advantage of children who cannot judge a commercial message small enough to justify the potential benefits of exposing children to educational entertainment? How vulnerable really are children to a sales pitch or the collection of personal contact data?

Chapter 3

1. Talent agents earn money by taking a percentage of what their clients earn; therefore it is to their advantage to place their clients in roles that earn as much money as possible. Whereas adult performers can discuss this potential conflict of interest directly, child performers, as legal minors, are one stage removed from negotiations about roles and contracts. Should extra safeguards—professional and/or legal—be in place to ensure that child performers are not harmed by their agents? Are parents and guardians adequate protection from unscrupulous agents?

2. According to Rebecca Ascher-Walsh, child performers are trained and nurtured by the studios that pay them; they represent a serious investment of production resources that the studio hopes will pay off in popularity and ticket sales. Do child performers who benefit from the development of their talent owe their studios more than adult performers who sign contracts after developing professional skills elsewhere? Are morality and behavior requirements (official or unspoken) an inappropriate intrusion of the studio into a child performer's life?

Chapter 4

1. Breaking into show business is hard work at any age, and requires a flexibility to take advantage of sudden opportunities that arise without much warning. Children trying to break into performing or acting rely on other people to transport them to these opportunities—other people who are usually busy working and taking care of other people. Is it fair to ask other family members, especially siblings, to make personal sacrifices for the performing child's fledgling career? Considering how unlikely it is that any performer will get a big break and develop a successful career, is it ever responsible for a parent to neglect attention to most of a family in order to chase the dreams of a single, dependent member?

2. One very important fact about child performers is that they are part of a family, and that the success or failure of a child is not just a personal triumph or burden. Is it unreasonable to expect that parents—even though they are supposed to be the mature adult who keeps a level head—remain aloof from the child's excitement about performing? Should parents ever take credit for any part of a child's success? Do you think that parents accused of hogging a child's limelight are ever just overly enthusiastic and misunderstood? What kinds of behaviors might indicate the difference?

Organizations to Contact

The editors have compiled the following list of organizations concerned with the issues debated in this book. The descriptions are derived from materials provided by the organizations. All have publications or information available for interested readers. The list was compiled on the date of publication of the present volume; the information provided here may change. Be aware that many organizations take several weeks or longer to respond to inquiries, so allow as much time as possible.

American Center for Children and Media (ACCM)
5400 North St. Louis Avenue, Chicago, IL 60625
(773) 509-5510 • fax: (773) 509-5303
e-mail: info@centerforchildrenandmedia.org
Web site: www.centerforchildrenandmedia.org

The American Center for Children and Media (ACCM) aims to support the children's media industry by developing, implementing, and promoting policies and practices that respect young people's well-being. Its goals are to accurately predict emerging business, social, technological and creative issues that will affect children's media; to produce objective research-based analyses of current issues and topics; and to establish a credible and effective voice for the industry.

A Minor Consideration
15003 S. Denker Avenue, Gardena, CA 90247-3113
fax: (310) 523-3691
Web site: www.minorcon.org

A Minor Consideration is a nonprofit, tax-deductible foundation dedicated to protecting the legal and human rights of juvenile performers in the entertainment industry as well as their financial security and their physical, mental, and emotional health. To this end, the foundation calls attention to child exploitation in all segments of popular entertainment and show business, and works with lawmakers to ensure that child labor laws are effective in protecting the welfare of these vulnerable young actors, singers, dancers, and athletes. Its goal is to make industry child labor laws uniform throughout the nation.

Association for Library Service to Children (ALSC)

50 East Huron, Chicago, IL   60611-2795
(800) 545-2433 x2163 • fax: (312) 280-5271
e-mail: alsc@ala.org
Web site: www.ala.org/alsc

The Association for Library Service to Children (ALSC) is a division of the American Library Association (ALA), a professional organization for librarians. The ALSC is dedicated to creating a better future for children through libraries. Its primary goal is to lead the way in forging excellent library service for all children.

BizParentz Foundation

PO Box 2477, Rancho Cucamonga, CA   91729
e-mail:bizinfo@bizparentz.org
Web site: www.bizparentz.org

The BizParentz Foundation is a nonprofit corporation providing education, advocacy, and charitable support to parents and children engaged in the entertainment industry. The organization promotes a positive public image regarding child performers and educates the public regarding the safety and rights of child performers, including child labor laws and regulations. BizParentz is a collaborative effort of parents, government, and industry organizations. Members actively help others by bringing legislative issues to the forefront, researching industry solutions, writing educational articles, and planning special events.

Campaign for a Commercial-Free Childhood (CCFC)

53 Parker Hill Avenue, Boston, MA   02120

(617) 278-4172 • fax: (617) 232-7343
e-mail: ccfc@jbcc.harvard.edu
Web site: www.commercialexploitation.org

The Campaign for a Commercial-Free Childhood (CCFC) is a national coalition of health care professionals, educators, advocacy groups, parents, and individuals who care about children. It is the only national organization devoted to limiting the impact of commercial culture on children. The CCFC's mission is to reclaim childhood from corporate marketers and works for the rights of children to grow up—and the freedom for parents to raise them—without being undermined by commercial interests. The CCFC advocates for the adoption of government policies that limit corporate marketers' access to children.

Children Now

1212 Broadway, 5th Floor, Oakland, CA   94612
(510) 763-2444 • fax: (510) 763-1974
e-mail: info@childrennow.org
Web site: www.childrennow.org

Children Now is a national organization that works toward ensuring children remain a top public policy priority. Its Children & the Media Program seeks a positive media environment for children. The organization conducts and publishes a variety of studies on media issues as well as reports focusing on children's education, child care, and health.

Christian Youth Theater (CYT)

1545 Pioneer Way, El Cajon, CA   92020
(800) 696-1929 • fax: (619) 588-4384
e-mail: info@cyt.org
Web site: www.cyt.org

The Christian Youth Theater (CYT) is an after-school theater arts training program for students from ages four to eighteen. Founded in 1981 in San Diego, California, CYT has grown to be the largest youth theater in the nation, with branches in cities across the United States. CYT offers theater arts classes for children as an after-school activity. Each local program conducts three ten-week sessions throughout the school year, teaching drama, voice, dance, and a broad spectrum of specialty theatrical workshops at weekly two-hour classes. Enrolled students have the opportunity to work behind the scenes, or audition and perform on stage in a Broadway-style musical performed for the community.

Entertainment Software Association (ESA)
575 Seventh Street NW, Suite 300, Washington, DC   20004
e-mail: esa@theesa.com
Web site: www.theesa.com

The Entertainment Software Association (ESA) is an association exclusively dedicated to serving the business and public affairs needs of companies that publish computer and video games. It offers a range of services to interactive entertainment software publishers, including a global antipiracy program, business and consumer research, government relations, and intellectual property protection efforts. The ESA also owns and operates the E3 Expo. In January 2000, the ESA board of directors authorized the creation of the ESA Foundation, which is dedicated to supporting positive programs and opportunities that will make a difference in the health, welfare, and quality of life of America's youth.

Federal Communications Commission, Media Bureau
445 Twelfth Street SW, Washington, DC   20554
(888) 225-5322 • fax: (866) 418-0232
e-mail: fccinfo@fcc.gov
Web site: www.fcc.gov

The Federal Communications Commission (FCC) is an independent U.S. government agency charged with regulating interstate and international communications by radio, television, wire, satellite, and cable. Its Media Bureau develops, recommends, and administers the policy and licensing programs relating to electronic media, and has a special division that focuses on children's television. Broadcasters are required to develop core programming for children according to educational and content guidelines developed by the FCC.

Henry J. Kaiser Family Foundation

2400 Sand Hill Road, Menlo Park, CA   94025
(650) 854-9400 • fax: (650) 854-4800
Web site: www.kff.org

The Henry J. Kaiser Family Foundation is a nonprofit, private operating foundation focusing on the major health care issues facing the United States. The foundation conducts research concerning the relationship between entertainment media and health, with a special focus on children and media, in order to provide data to help inform policy makers, journalists, the research community, health care providers, the media industry, and the public. Projects of the Kaiser Family Foundation include research on how teens use the Internet for health information; the amount of time children of all ages spend watching TV, playing video games, using computers, and reading; sexual messages on television; and the role of media in childhood obesity.

Parents Television Council (PTC)

707 Wilshire Boulevard, Suite 2075, Los Angeles, CA   90017
(213) 403-1300
e-mail: editor@parentstv.org
Web site: www.parentstv.org

Parents Television Council (PTC) was established as a special project of the Media Research Center. Its goal is to bring America's demand for values-driven television programming to the entertainment industry. PTC produces the annual *Family Guide to Prime Time Television*, based on scientific monitoring and analysis generated from the Media Research Center's computerized media tracking system. The guide profiles every sitcom and drama on the major television networks and provides information on subject matter that is inappropriate for children. PTC also publishes various reports and a monthly newsletter, entitled *Insider*.

Screen Actors Guild Young Performers Committee
5757 Wilshire Boulevard, 7th Floor
Los Angeles, CA   90036-3600
(323) 954-1600
e-mail: saginfo@sag.org
Web site: www.sag.org

The Screen Actors Guild (SAG) is a labor organization whose mission is to negotiate the best possible wages and working conditions for professional actors. The Young Performers Committee provides information to child actors and their parents and guardians on how to establish and develop a career in television and movies. Members of SAG pay dues, but they receive protection as laborers and industry resources in return. Younger actors also benefit from the oversight of an official SAG representative when they are working on a set to ensure that rules and regulations about their safety, education requirements, and hours worked are followed.

TrueChild
1731 Connecticut Avenue NW, 4th Floor
Washington, DC   20009
(202) 462-6610 • fax: (202) 462-6744
e-mail: info@truechild.org
Web site: www.truechild.org

TrueChild is a national organization helping children break through stereotypes and allowing them to be true to themselves and reach their full potential. The organization advocates improving children's culture by holding the media accountable for the messages it sends to children and providing parents with information about the content of children's programming. It publishes a free monthly electronic newsletter and produces annual report cards on children's television programs.

Bibliography of Books

Daniel S. Acuff and Robert H. Reiher — *Kidnapped: How Irresponsible Marketers Are Stealing the Minds of Your Children*. Chicago, IL: Dearborn Publishing, 2005.

Martin Ashley — *How High Should Boys Sing? Gender, Authenticity and Credibility in the Young Male Voice*. Farnham, England: Ashgate Publishing, 2009.

Sharon Beder, Wendy Varney, and Richard Gosden — *This Little Kiddy Went to Market: The Corporate Capture of Childhood*. Sydney, Australia: University of New South Wales Press, 2009.

Mary Lou Belli and Dinah Lenney — *Acting for Young Actors: The Ultimate Teen Guide*. New York: Back Stage Books, 2006.

M. Gigi Durham — *The Lolita Effect: The Media Sexualization of Young Girls and What We Can Do About It*. Woodstock, NY: Overlook Press, 2008.

Lisa Gee — *Stage Mum: When Showbiz Happens to Your Child*. London: Arrow, 2009.

Lisa Guernsey — *Into the Minds of Babes: How Screen Time Affects Children from Birth to Age Five*. New York: Basic Books, 2007.

Jessica Hopper — *The Girls' Guide to Rocking: How to Start a Rock Band, Book Gigs, and Get Rolling to Rock Stardom.* New York: Workman Publishing, 2009.

David Hutchison — *Playing to Learn: Video Games in the Classroom.* Westport, CT: Libraries Unlimited/Teacher Ideas Press, 2007.

Lisa Jacobson, ed. — *Children and Consumer Culture in American Society: A Historical Handbook and Guide.* Westport, CT: Praeger Publishers, 2008.

Roger J.R. Levesque — *Adolescents, Media, and the Law: What Developmental Science Reveals and Free Speech Requires.* New York: Oxford University Press, 2007.

Diane E. Levin and Jean Kilbourne — *So Sexy So Soon: The New Sexualized Childhood and What Parents Can Do to Protect Their Kids.* New York: Ballantine Books, 2008.

Martin Lindström with Patricia B. Seybold — *Brand Child: Remarkable Insights into the Minds of Today's Global Kids and Their Relationships with Brands.* London: Kogan Page, 2003.

Susan Linn — *The Case for Make Believe: Saving Play in a Commercialized World.* New York: New Press, 2008.

Robert W. Morrow — *Sesame Street and the Reform of Children's Television.* Baltimore, MD: Johns Hopkins University Press, 2006.

Sharon L. Nichols and Thomas L. Good

America's Teenagers—Myths and Realities: Media Images, Schooling, and the Social Costs of Careless Indifference. Mahwah, NJ: Lawrence Erlbaum Associates, 2004.

Jane C. O'Connor

The Cultural Significance of the Child Star. New York: Routledge, 2008.

Deborah O'Keefe

Good Girl Messages: How Young Women Were Misled by Their Favorite Books. New York: Continuum, 2001.

Nicholas Sammond

Babes in Tomorrowland: Walt Disney and the Making of the American Child, 1930–1960. Durham, NC: Duke University Press, 2005.

Jeff Share

Media Literacy Is Elementary: Teaching Youth to Critically Read and Create Media. New York: Peter Lang, 2009.

Gregory S. Smith

How to Protect Your Children on the Internet: A Roadmap for Parents and Teachers. Westport, CT: Praeger Publishers, 2007.

Victor C. Strasburger, Barbara J. Wilson, and Amy B. Jordan

Children, Adolescents, and the Media. Los Angeles, CA: Sage, 2009.

Michelle Vogel

Children of Hollywood: Accounts of Growing Up as the Sons and Daughters of Stars. Jefferson, NC: McFarland & Company, 2005.

Index